About the Author

Irene Daria, Ph.D. is a developmental psychologist who specializes in teaching children how to read.

In addition to teaching the children of many celebrities to read, she has taught hundreds of other children—both as a paid specialist and as a volunteer—and has trained teachers in the science of reading.

A passionate literacy advocate, Dr. Daria is the founder and director of Steps Tutoring in New York City. Her *Steps to Reading* workbook series will enable you to teach a child how to read using the same research-based, fun, and effective methods Dr. Daria uses in her renown private lessons.

For more information, visit:
www.StepsTutoring.com or www.StepstoReading.com.

Discounts available for bulk orders and orders meant for educational use. Email Purchase Director at info@StepsPublishing.com. For more information see...

www.StepstoReading.com

Printed in the U.S.A.
ISBN 979-8-9904934-0-7

Book 1

ST🔲PS to...
Reading

by Irene Daria, Ph.D.

Illustrations by Tingting Wei, Eryka Sajek, and Eric Wiener

Table of Contents

Supplemental Materials

In a very short time, children using this book will be able to read actual stories all by themselves. The books below are optional but highly recommended. I will be referring you to these stories as the child progresses through this book. They will reinforce the lessons in this book, and the child will be so excited to be able to read them!

- "Bob Books, Set 1," by Bobby Lynn Maslin. This is a boxed set of 12 very short, very easy stories. Published by Scholastic.

- "Primary Phonics Storybooks Set 1," by Barbara Makar. This is a set of 10 lovely, decodable stories. Published by Educators Publishing Service.

For free, supplemental, decodable passages, go to StepstoReading.com and click on "resources."

Short vowels

a says /ă/ as in

i says /ĭ/ as in

u says /ŭ/ as in

e says /ĕ/ as in

o says /ŏ/ as in

This book teaches children the short vowel sounds. "Short" refers to the sound vowels make in words like "cat," "him," "bus," "hen," and "hot." The short vowel sound is represented by a semicircle symbol ⌣ placed over the vowel like so: /ă/

Instructions

1. Say to the child: **"Today we are going to learn the sound that** a **makes. That sound is /ǎ/ as in apple or ant."**

2. Go to www.starfall.com.* Make sure your computer's sound is turned on.

3. Click on "Kindergarten and Pre-K." Then, at the top of the screen, click on the alphabet blocks labeled "ABCs." More alphabet blocks will appear.

4. Click on the alphabet block for the letter a .

5. When you are done watching the presentation for the first screen, tell the child to click on the sparkling stars to get to the next screen.

6. Every so often, as the child progresses through the activity, ask, **"What sound does** a **make?"** The child should respond by making the short /ǎ/ sound.

7. After the child has done the a activity, click on the ⓐ circle at the bottom of the screen and listen to the song. When it is done, the website will ask you if you want to listen to the song again. I recommend listening to the song as often as possible and singing it when you are away from the computer.

Starfall.com is the best website out there for beginning readers. I have no affiliation with this website or with any books I recommend that you get for your child to read.

a a a

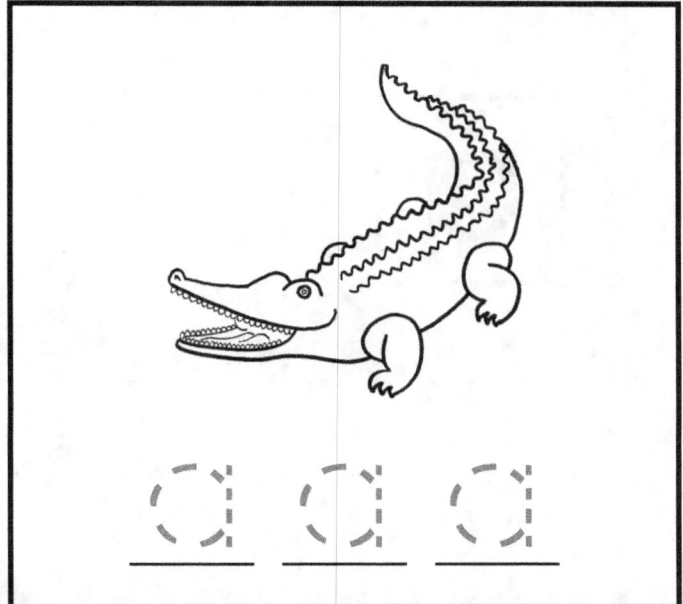

a a a

a a a

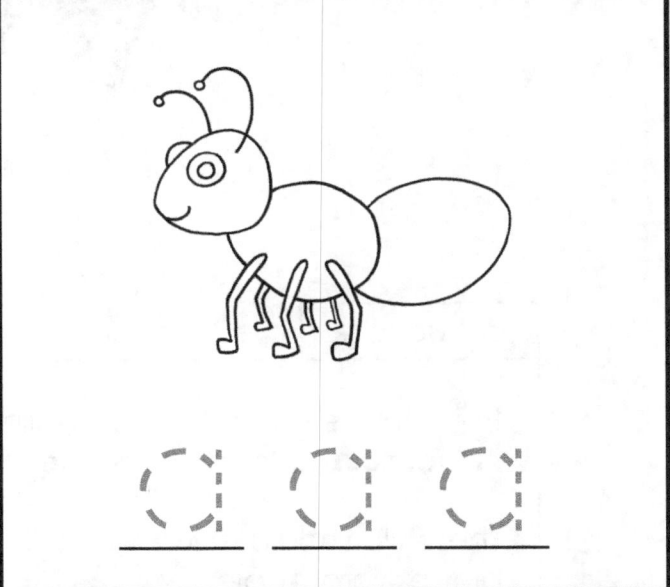

a a a

Instructions

Say to the child: "**The letter** a **makes the /ă/ sound, as in 'apple.'**"
1. Have the child color in each picture and trace the letters below it.
2. Each time he or she finishes coloring in a picture, say, "**What sound does** a **make?**" The child should make the /ă/ sound.
3. Each time he or she finishes tracing a set of three letters, say, "**What sound does** a **make?**" The child should make the /ă/ sound.

Separate letters make separate sounds

Instructions

Point to the letter a in the illustration above, and ask the child, **"What sound does a make?"**

The child should make the short / ă / sound, as in the beginning of the word apple.

Point to the letter t in the illustration above, and say, **"What sound does t make?"**

The child should make the / t / sound, as in the beginning of the word tap.

Say: **"When letters stand alone, or are far apart from each other, each letter will make its own sound."**

Instructions

Say: "**When** a **and** t **stand side by side, their sounds combine to make a word!**"

Point to the word at in the illustration above, and say, "**This word is** at **, as in, 'I will meet you** at **the park,' or 'The car stopped** at **the corner.'**"

Say: "**Now you read it.**"

The child should say, "at."

Play the "at" board game

First one to reach the end wins!

Instructions

<u>Materials you will need</u>:
- A single die.
- Coins to use as markers.
- Gameboard, *opposite page.*

1. Each player places a coin on "start."
2. Take turns rolling the die.
3. Move forward the same amount of spaces as the number on the die.
4. As you move forward on the board, make the sound of the letter, or read the word, that you pass, as well as the one you land on.
5. For example, if a five comes up on the die, move five spaces on the game board and read five words and/or sounds.
6. Assist the child as much as is necessary, until he is able to read the words/sounds on his own.
7. The first person to reach the end wins the game.

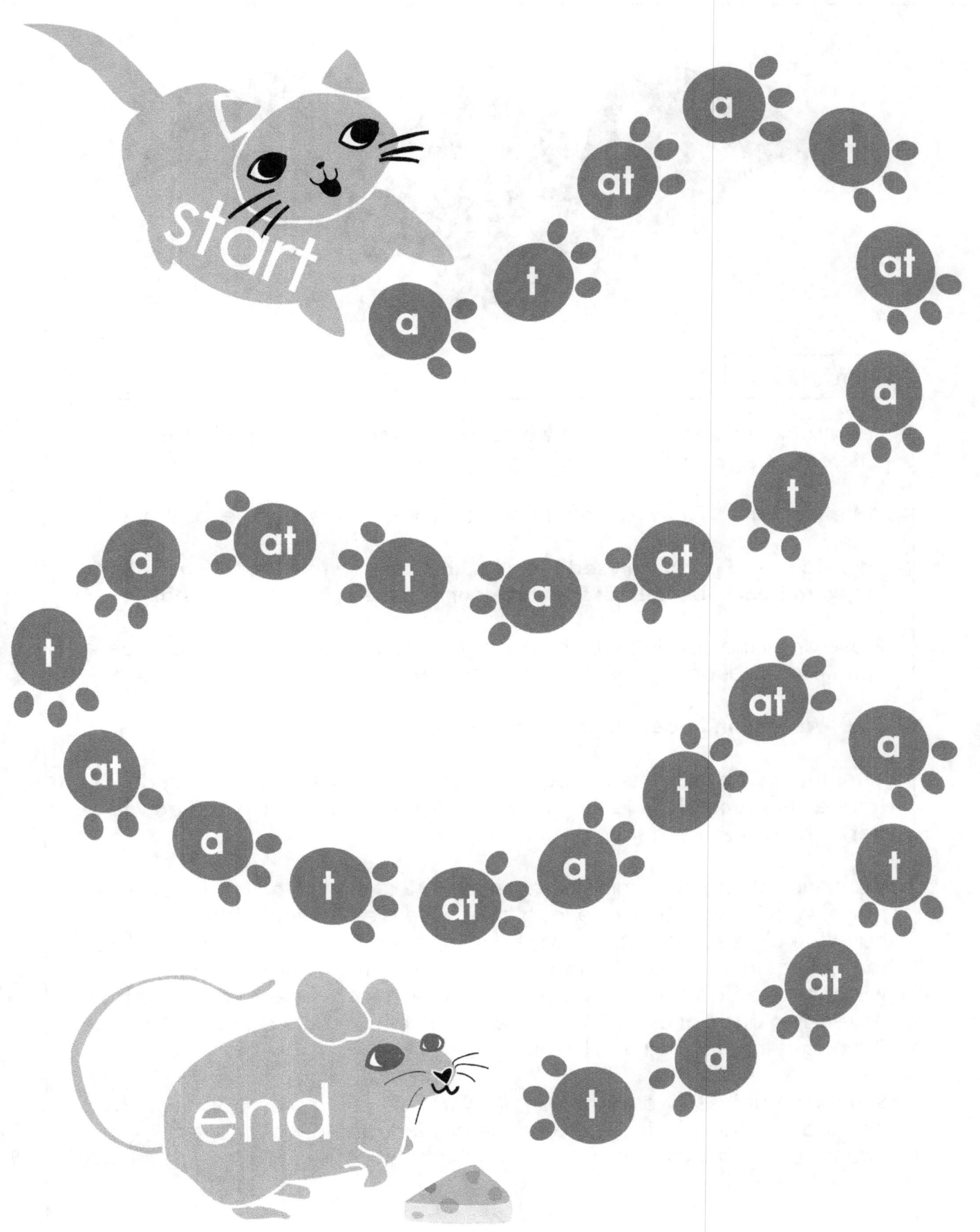

Step 2

Instructions

Say: "**Look how many different words we can make just by putting a different letter in front of the word 'at.'**"

Write the letter 'b' in front of the first __at word, *opposite page*, as shown.

Say: "**This word is 'bat.' It used to be 'at,' but after I wrote the 'b' on the line, the word became 'bat!' Let's sound it out together: /b/.../ă/.../t/...bat.**"

Move on to the next letter in the box at the bottom of the opposite page. Write that letter on the line in front of the next __at word.

Say: "**What sound does this letter make?**"

After the child makes the correct sound, say, "**When we put the sound (make the sound of the letter you wrote) in front of 'at', what word do we get?**" The child should sound out the word.

Continue with the remaining letters in the letter box, *bottom of the opposite page*. Working with one letter at a time, write the letter on a blank line, and have the child sound out the word. It is important for you, the teacher, to do the writing on the opposite page. It is very effective for the child to see the words be created before her eyes. On this page, all her energy should be on reading and not on writing. However, the child should do the writing on the pages that follow in this lesson.

Sounding out these words may be tricky at first. Help the child as much as needed until she gets it. Every time the child reads the word correctly, praise her. This is really a great accomplishment for the child, and she should feel very proud.

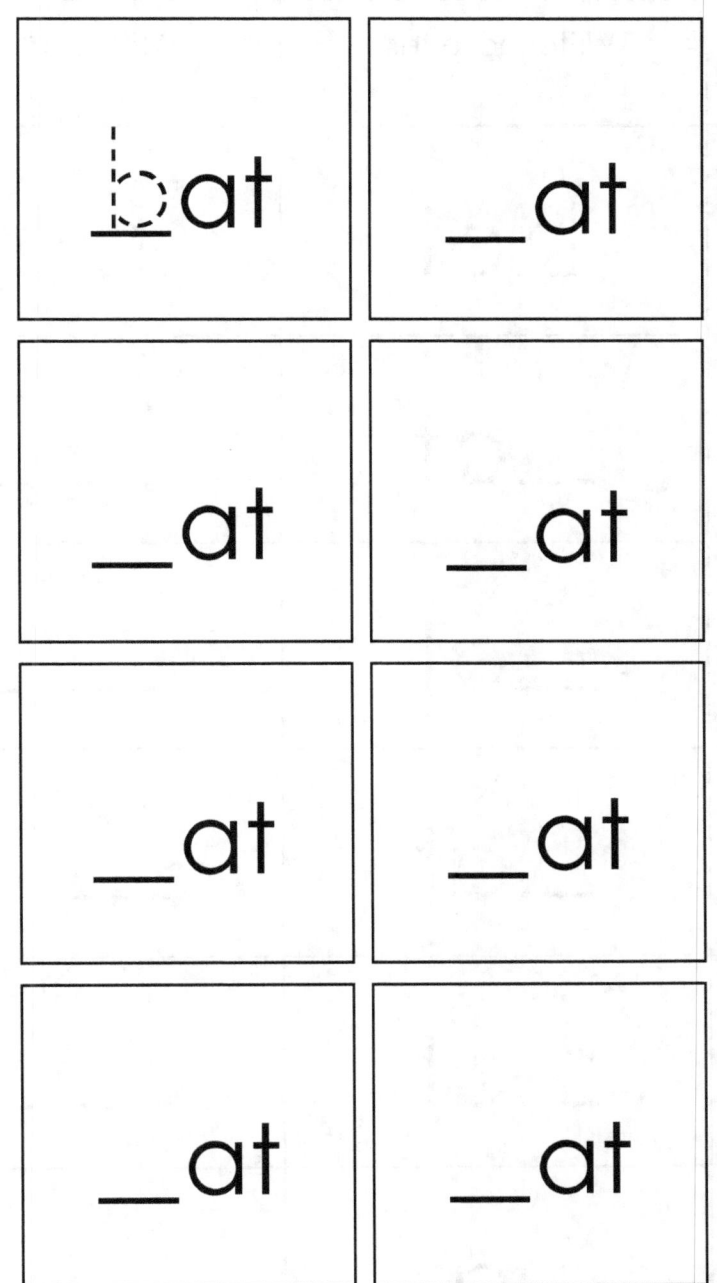

Teacher: Write these letters on the lines above.

b, c, h, f, m, r, s, p

Write and read the word

Read the instructions, *below*, to the child. The child should do the sounding out and the writing.

Sound out ↓	Write the letter ↓	Write and read the word ↓
b	bat	b a t
c	_at	__ __ __ __
h	_at	__ __ __ __
f	_at	__ __ __ __
m	_at	__ __ __ __
r	_at	__ __ __ __
s	_at	__ __ __ __

Write the word and circle the picture

Say: "**Read the word out loud. Then write it, and circle the picture that shows the word.**"

cat

___ ___ ___

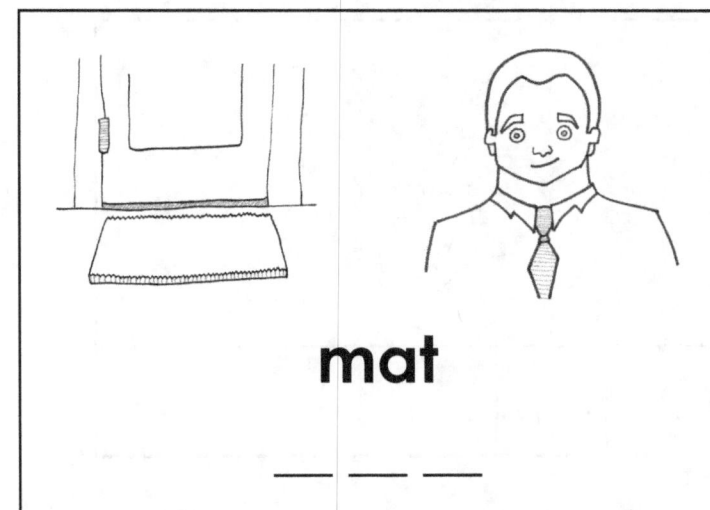

mat

___ ___ ___

bat

___ ___ ___

hat

___ ___ ___

sat

___ ___ ___

rat

___ ___ ___

Circle the letters

Say: "**Circle the correct letters. Then write the word.**"

b (b) m | (a) p | r | (t)   b a t

m h | p a | r t   _ _ _ _

c d | f a | t g   _ _ _ _

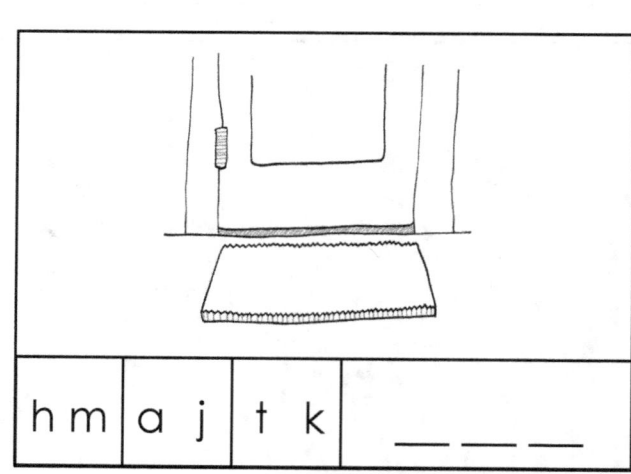

h m | a j | t k   _ _ _ _

s r | v a | t b   _ _ _ _

s g | a h | t k   _ _ _ _

Play Bingo with words that end in "at'

Bingo!

Instructions

Materials: • Flashcards. Cut out the cards that follow.
• 2 gameboards. In Bingo, every player gets his own game board. You and the child should each take one of the gameboards. (Order the flashcards so the child wins often!)
• Pennies or other small items to use as game pieces.

1. Place the flashcards in one stack, with the words facing up.
2. Have the child read the word on the top card in the stack.
3. Each of you should look for that word on your Bingo boards and place a penny on top of the word on your boards when you find it.
4. Place the card the child read face down on the table.
5. Repeat steps 2-4. The child should be the one doing all of the reading of the words on the flashcards. Continue until one of you has three pennies in a row, either horizontally, vertically, or diagonally. The first player to get three in a row should call out, "Bingo!" That player wins the game.

This page is intentionally left blank.

Bingo Flashcards

Cut out the cards along the dotted lines.

cat	fat	sat
mat	at	pat
bat	rat	hat

This page is intentionally left blank.

This page is intentionally left blank.

BINGO

bat	sat	mat
at	pat	cat
hat	fat	rat

BINGO

cat	fat	sat
mat	at	pat
bat	rat	hat

This page is intentionally left blank.

What you need to know about...
Power Words

Back in 1936, a professor named Edward William Dolch came up with a list of the 220 most frequently used words in the English language.

Those words came to be referred to as "sight words" because teachers wanted children to immediately recognize the words "on sight," as opposed to sound them out. Many parents believe sight words don't follow phonics rules and, so, need to be memorized. Actually, many sight words do follow phonics rules. For example: and, is, in, that. Others do not follow the rules. For example: the, said.

In time, Dolch divided his list according to grade levels, and the words on each of those lists were listed in alphabetical order. This was unfortunate because it meant that children were learning how to read "brown" before they knew how to read "said," even though "said" appears much more often in stories than the word "brown." To this day, sight words are typically introduced in an order that has nothing to do with the stories children are trying to read. In addition, many experts feel that it is unnecessary to have kids memorize so many sight words since they will soon know how to sound them out. That's why I put together my own list of what I call Power Words.

This book introduces Power Words in their order of frequency of use. Some of the Power Words do not follow phonics rules. Some of them do, but they are rules the child has not yet learned. Learning these Power Words will enable children to read sentences and stories starting at the very earliest stages of instruction.

Power Word

Instructions

1. Say: "**Some words don't follow any of the sounding-out rules. They are words that just need to be memorized. We will call them 'power words' because they are words that appear very often in the stories you will soon be reading. Knowing these words will really boost your reading power. The first of these words is 'the.'**"

2. Point to the word 'the' on the top line on the opposite page. Say, "**Trace the word 'the.' Then write it four times next to the one you traced.**"

3. Repeat until the child has completed the whole sheet.

4. Any time you come to a Power Word in this book, read the word to the child and have him trace and write the word on the lines that follow.

Write the Word

the

the

the

the

the

the

23

Instructions

1. Say: "**So far we've sounded out words that end in** at **. Now we're going to sound out words that end in** an **. 'An' is a word all by itself too. For example, you would use it in the sentence, 'I would like an apple.'**"

2. Point to the word an in the box above.

3. Say, "**When** a **and** n **are side by side, they make the word** an **. You read it.**"

4. The child should say, "An."

---

1. *Opposite page:* Say, "**Look how many different words we can make just by putting a different letter in front of the word** an **.**"

2. Write the letter "c" on the line in front of the first __an, as shown.

3. Say: "**This word is 'can.' It used to be** an **, but after I wrote the 'c' on the line, the word became 'can!'**"

4. Continue with the remaining letters in the letter box, *bottom of the opposite page*. Working with one letter at a time, write the letter on a blank line, and have the child sound out the word. You, the teacher, should do the writing so the child can focus on watching the words be created.

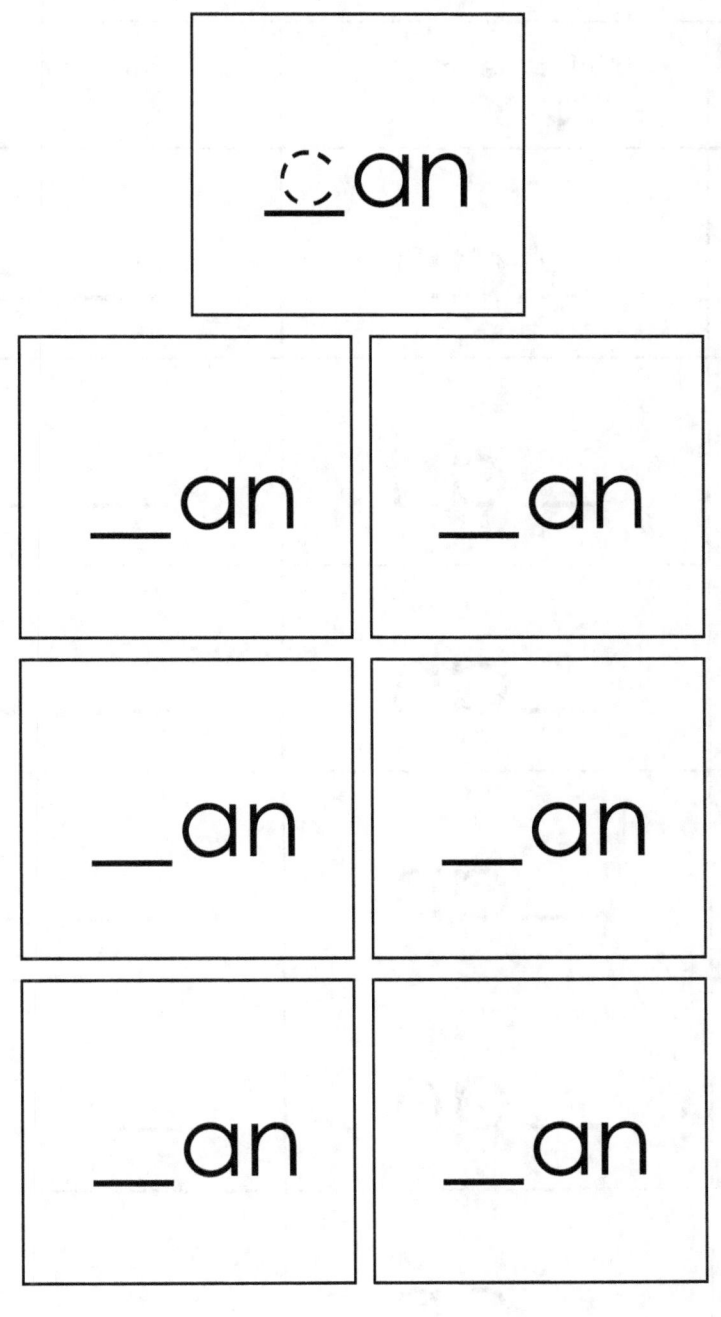

can

__an   __an

__an   __an

__an   __an

Teacher: Write these letters on the lines above.

c, f, m, p, r, t, v

Write and read the word

Read the instructions, *below*, to the child. The child should do the sounding out and the writing.

Sound out ↓	Write the letter ↓	Write and read the word ↓
v	v an	v a n
m	_an	_ _ _ _
p	_an	_ _ _ _
f	_an	_ _ _ _
c	_an	_ _ _ _
r	_an	_ _ _ _
t	_an	_ _ _ _

Say: "**Read each word out loud. Circle the word that goes with the picture.**"

cat   can

bat   ban

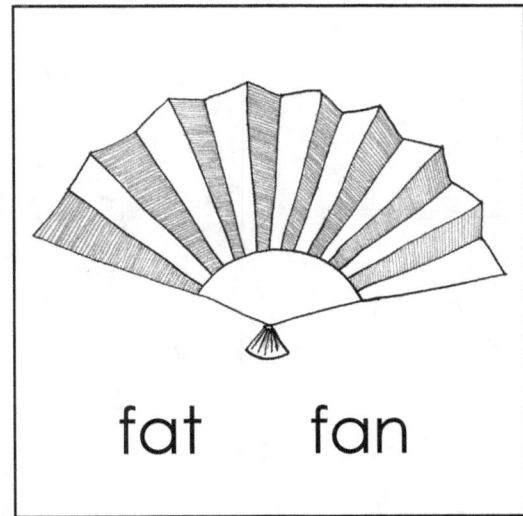

fat   fan

rat   ran

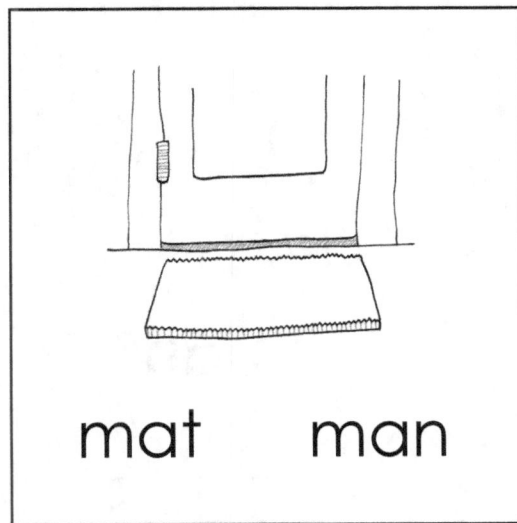

mat   man

pat   pan

Write the word and circle the picture

Say: "Read the word out loud. Then write the word, and circle the picture that shows the word."

pan

— — —

ran

— — —

van

— — —

man

— — —

can

— — —

fan

— — —

Say: "**You are doing so well! Guess what? You can read sentences now! Read these to me.**" (Point to each word in the sentences below as the child reads.)

The rat sat.

Pat the cat.

The bat sat.

The cat sat.

Pat the man.

Say: "**Great job!**" The child just took a really big step. I recommend celebrating in a small way that feels right for you and the child.

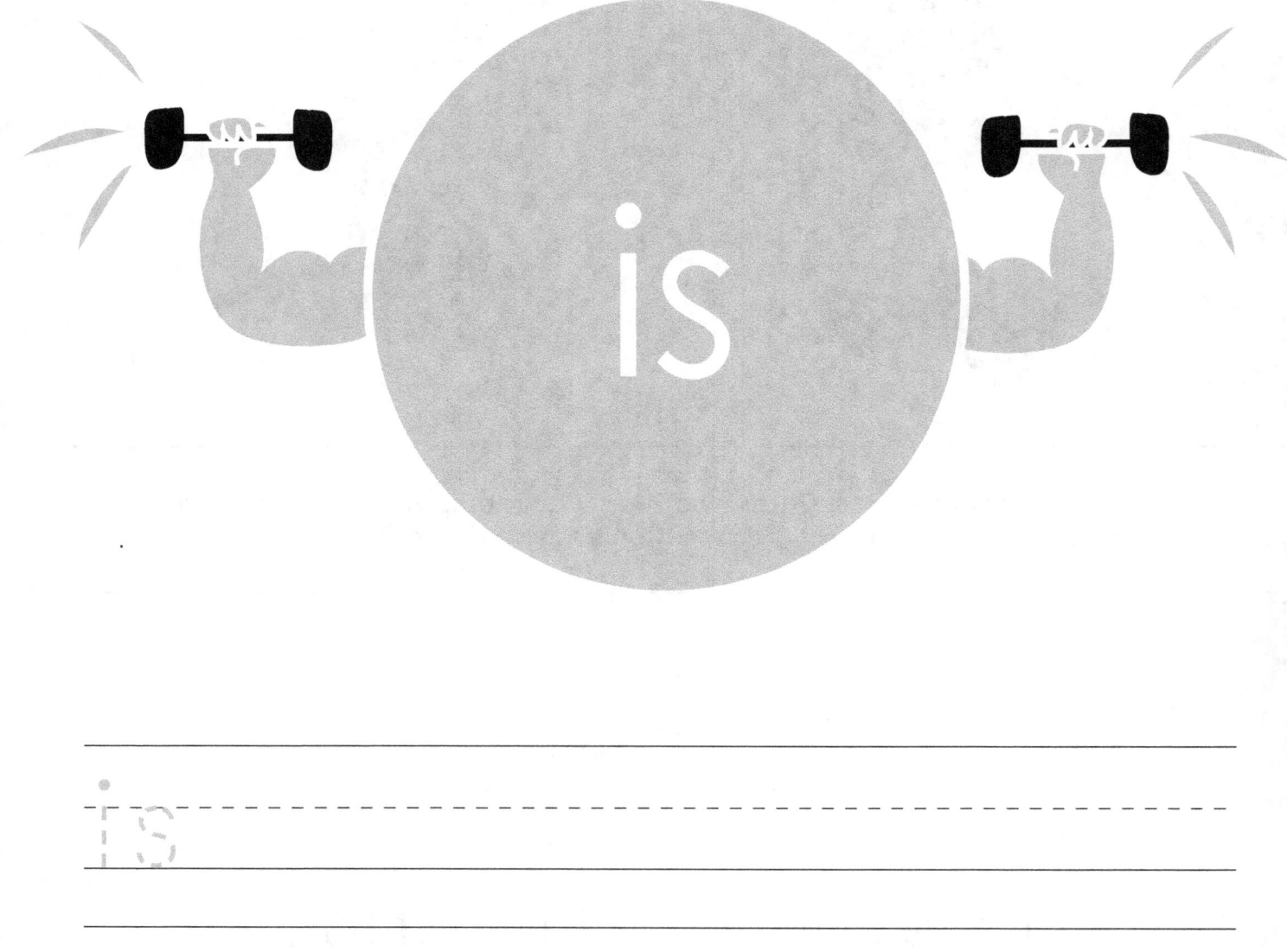

is

is

is

is

Play Bingo!

The Bingo game on the following pages reinforces short "a" words that end in "n" and "t." Cut out the flashcards on this page, grab a handful of pennies and you are all set to play. If you need a refresher on game instructions, see page 13.

fat	ran	fan
mat	cat	man
pan	rat	can

This page is intentionally left blank.

This page is intentionally left blank.

BINGO

cat	rat	fan
ran	can	mat
man	pan	fat

BINGO

fat	ran	fan
mat	cat	man
pan	rat	can

This page is intentionally left blank.

Silly Sentences

Instructions

1. Cut out the words on the opposite page.
2. Place all the words face up on a table. Put the power words on the left side and the words ending in "at" or "an" on the right.
3. Say: "**We are going to make sentences today. Choose any words that you want. Line the words up next to each other so they make a sentence. The sentence can be a real sentence, or it can be a silly one. I'll go first.**"
4. Choose words to make the following sentence: "The pan is on the man." Place the words next to each other in the correct order.
5. Say: "**The pan is on the man. That's a silly sentence, isn't it?**"
6. Then say, "**Now it's your turn. Make a sentence, and then read it to me.**"
7. Take turns making sentences and then reading them out loud. Do this for as long as the activity is fun for the child. Most kids get a big kick out of the silly sentences.

can	fan	man	hat	van
can	fan	man	hat	van
cat	bat	fat	pat	sat
cat	bat	fat	pat	sat
the	is	on	pan	rat
The	is	on	pan	rat
The	the	on	mat	tan
The	the	is	mat	tan

This page is intentionally left blank.

Circle the letters

Say: "Circle the correct letters. Then write the word.
Notice that just changing the last letter makes a totally different word."

| v | c | b | a | n | f | c a n → |
| c | d | | f | a | t | g | ____ |

| b | f | a | g | n | h | ____ → |
| m | f | a | k | e | t | ____ |

| m | c | a | j | k | n | ____ → |
| h | m | a | j | t | k | ____ |

| t | r | w | a | n | d | ____ → |
| r | c | f | a | h | t | ____ |

Instructions

1. Say: "**You've mastered words that end in** t **and** n . **Now we're going to sound out words that end in** am , **as in, 'I am going to the park today.'**"

2. Point to the word am in the box above.

3. Say, "**When** a **and** m **are side by side, they make the word** am . **You read it.**"

4. The child should say, "Am."

---

1. *Opposite page:* Say, "**Look how many different words we can make just by putting a different letter in front of the word** am ."

2. Write the letter 'b' on the line in front of the first __am, as shown.

3. Say: "**This word is 'bam.' It used to be** am , **but after I wrote the 'b' on the line, the word became 'bam!'**"

4. Continue with the remaining letters in the letter box, *bottom of opposite page*. Working with one letter at a time, write the letter on one of the blank lines on the opposite page, and have the child sound out the word. You, the teacher, should do the writing so the child can focus on watching the words be created.

Make words that end in "am"

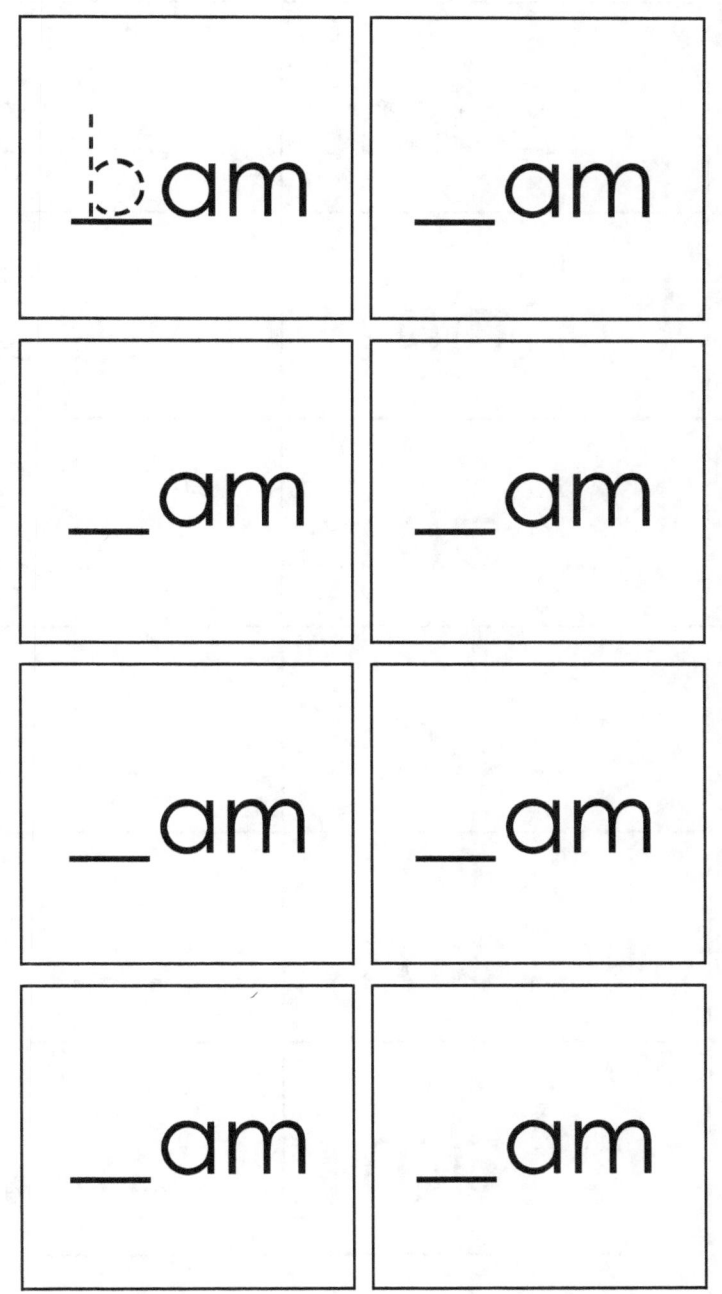

Teacher: Write these letters on the lines above.
b, d, h, j, r, y, P, S

Write and read the word

Sound out ↓	Write the letter ↓	Write and read the word ↓
S	Sam	S a m
j	_am	__ __ __
b	_am	__ __ __
y	_am	__ __ __
h	_am	__ __ __
r	_am	__ __ __
P	_am	__ __ __
d	_am	__ __ __

Say: "**You know how to sound out words that end in t, n and m!**
Now let's sound out words that end in g."

Sound out	Write the letter	Write and read the word
b	bag	b a g
l	_ag	___ ___ ___
n	_ag	___ ___ ___
r	_ag	___ ___ ___
s	_ag	___ ___ ___
t	_ag	___ ___ ___
w	_ag	___ ___ ___

Write the word and circle the picture

Say: Read the word out loud, then write it and circle the picture that shows the word.

bag

___ ___ ___

wag

___ ___ ___

bat

___ ___ ___

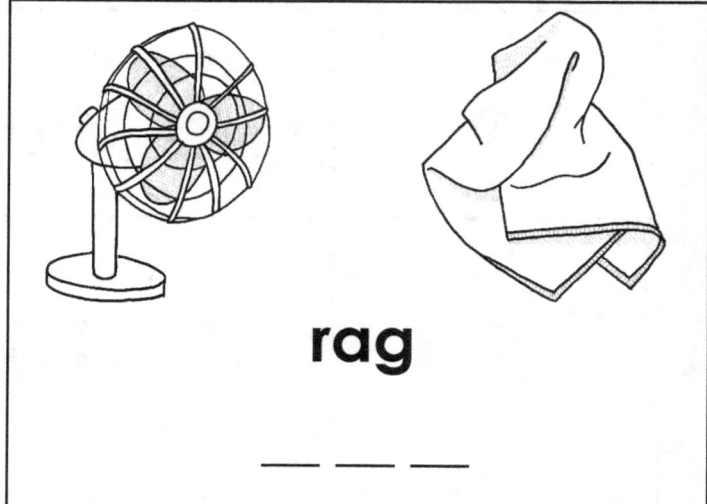

rag

___ ___ ___

tag

___ ___ ___

can

___ ___ ___

Draw a line from the word to the picture

Say: "**Read each word out loud. Then draw a line from the correct word to the picture.**"

can
cat
sag

bat
tan
jam

bag
pan
hat

Sam
nag
ran

ham
fan
lag

man
wag
fat

You can read a book!

Instructions

Say: "**Guess what? You can read a book now!**" Have the child read "Mat." This is Book 1 in "Bob Books, Set 1." See page i ("Supplemental Materials") for more information.

The book is very short and very easy and very much a milestone! Wait until you see the look on the child's face when he or she realizes he or she can read it! Take a few minutes to celebrate. Make this step feel like a real accomplishment for the child because it is!

<u>NOTE</u>: The child will also be able to read Book 2 ("Sam") in the "Bob Books, Set 1." Save "Sam" for the next day you are able to work with the child. It's important not to overdo things at this early stage of reading. A sense of accomplishment can very easily turn into a sense of frustration if the child gets tired. Also, a little bit of work every day is much more effective than a lot of work every few days.

After the child reads "Sam," celebrate again. Then move on to the next lesson in this workbook.

Play Bingo!

This Bingo game reinforces short "a" words that end in various letters. Cut out the flashcards on this page and have fun! (The big X in the center of the gameboards that follow is a "free" space. Each of you can use that space on your boards to get five in a row.)

Sam	fat	at	tan

cat	hat	mat	sad	bat
ham	can	mad	bag	rag
ran	rat	had	wag	am
man	sag	pan	cab	van

This page is intentionally left blank.

This page is intentionally left blank.

BINGO

cat	hat	mat	sad	bat
ham	can	mad	bag	rag
ran	rat	✕	wag	am
man	sag	pan	cab	van
Sam	fat	at	tan	had

BINGO

cat	can	cab	had	hat
ham	mat	mad	sad	bag
bat	rag	✕	ran	rat
wag	am	Sam	man	mat
pan	van	at	fat	tan

This page is intentionally left blank.

as
has

as

as

has

has

Vocabulary

ban

To make something illegal.
Example: **The town will ban fishing in the lake.**

bam

A loud noise.
Example: **The bookcase toppled over with a bam.**

dam

A wall that holds back water.
Example: **The water overflowed the dam.**

ram

To hit hard.
Example: **If you do not stop the car, you will ram into the car in front of you.**

yam

A sweet potato that is orange in color.
Example: **The yam was delicious.**

lag

To fall behind.
Example: **If you do not walk with the group, you will lag behind the group.**

You can read more stories!

Instructions

Read a book

The child should read: "Mac and Tab," by Barbara Makar. This is Book 1 in "Primary Phonics, Set 1." See page i ("Supplemental Materials") for more information.

Read online

1. Go to www.starfall.com.
2. Click on "Kindergarten" and then on the second item in the center (Language Arts) menu. It is called "Learn to Read."
3. Click on "Zac the Rat" in the column that says, "Book." Make sure the computer's sound is on.
4. Tell the child to read the sentence that appears on the screen for each page. Don't let him click on the individual words because, if he does, the computer will read the words for him. You want the child to do all the reading. After he is done reading each sentence, he can click on the picture above it. The picture will then move in a delightful way.

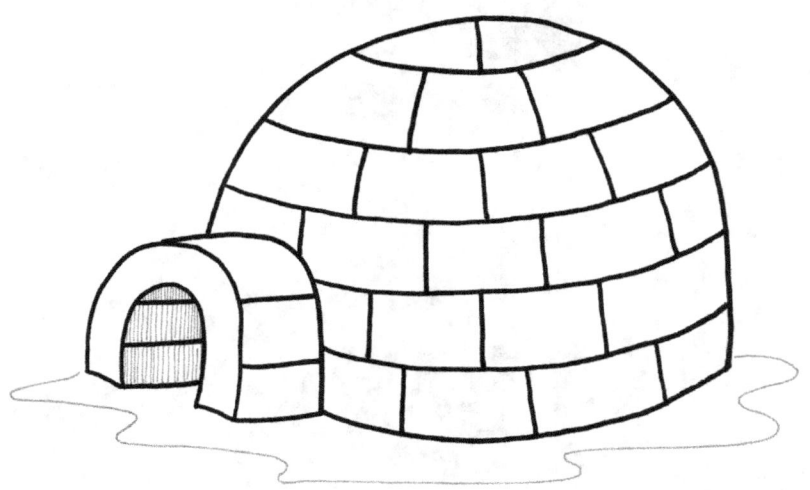

Instructions

1. Say: "**Now we're going to learn the sound ⟨i⟩ makes. ⟨i⟩ makes the /ĭ/ sound as in 'igloo,' 'it,' and 'hit.' Let's listen to it on the computer.**"

2. Go to www.starfall.com. Click on "Kindergarten and pre-K," then on the "ABCs" icon at the top left of the page.

3. Click on the alphabet block for the letter ⟨i⟩. Every so often, as the child progresses through the activity, ask, "**What sound does ⟨i⟩ make?**"

4. The child should respond by making the short /ĭ/ sound.

5. After the child has done the ⟨i⟩ activity, click on the ⓘ circle at the bottom of the screen and listen to the song. When it is done, the website will ask you if you want to listen to the song again. I recommend listening to the song as often as possible and singing it when you are away from the computer.

h i t

d i g

p i g

s i t

Instructions

Say: "**The letter** $\boxed{i}$ **makes the /ĭ/ sound, as in 'igloo.'**"
1. Have the child color in each picture and trace the word below it.
2. Each time he or she finishes coloring in a picture, say, "**What sound does** $\boxed{i}$ **make?**" The child should make the /ĭ/ sound.
3. Each time he or she finishes tracing a word, say, "**What sound does** $\boxed{i}$ **make?**" The child should make the /ĭ/ sound.

Words that end in "it"

Instructions

1. Point to the word it in the box above.

2. Say, "**When i and t are side by side, they make the word it . You read it.**"

3. The child should say, "It."

---

1. *Opposite page*: Say, "**Look how many different words we can make just by putting a different letter in front of the word it .**"

2. Write the letter "b" on the line in front of the first __it, as shown.

3. Say: "**This word is 'bit.' It used to be it , but after I wrote the 'b' on the line, the word became 'bit!'**"

4. Continue with the remaining letters in the letter box, *bottom of the opposite page*. Working with one letter at a time, write the letter on a blank line, and have the child sound out the word. You, the teacher, should do the writing so the child can focus on watching the words be created.

5. Remember to fill in one line at a time. Then have the child read the word. Don't fill in the whole page at once. Breaking things up into little steps makes it less intimidating for the child.

Make words that end in "it"

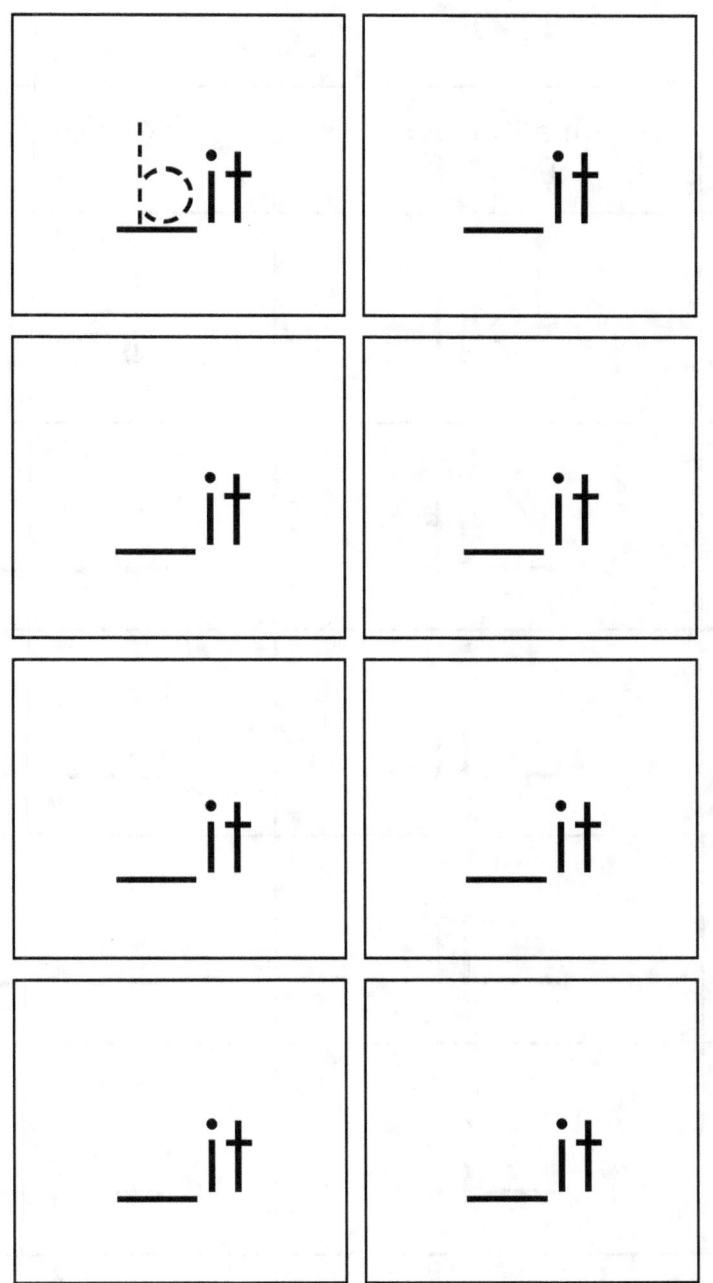

Teacher: Write these letters on the lines above.
Help the child sound out each word.

b, f, h, k, l, p, s, w

Write words that end in "it"

Read the instructions, *below*, to the child. The child should do the sounding out and the writing.

Sound out ↓	Write the letter ↓	Write and read the word ↓
b	bit	b i t
f	_it	_ _ _ _
p	_it	_ _ _ _
l	_it	_ _ _ _
k	_it	_ _ _ _
h	_it	_ _ _ _
s	_it	_ _ _ _

Draw a line from the word to the picture

fit
bit
hit

hit
pit
fit

lit
sit
kit

pit
lit
sit

sit
lit
fit

kit
hit
pit

Instructions

1. Point to the word in in the box above.

2. Say, "**When i and n are side by side, they make the word in .
You read it.**"

3. The child should say, "In."

4. *Opposite page*: Say, "**Look how many different words we can make just
by putting a different letter in front of the word in .**"

5. Write the letter "b" on the line in front of the first __in, as shown.

6. Say: "**This word is 'bin.' It used to be in , but after I wrote the 'b' on the
line, the word became 'bin!'**"

7. Continue with the remaining letters in the letter box, *bottom of the oppo-site page*. Working with one letter at a time, write the letter on a blank line,
and have the child sound out the word. You, the teacher, should do the
writing so the child can focus on watching the words be created.

8. Remember to fill in one line at a time. Then have the child read the word.
Don't fill in the whole page at once. Breaking things up into little steps
makes it less intimidating for the child.

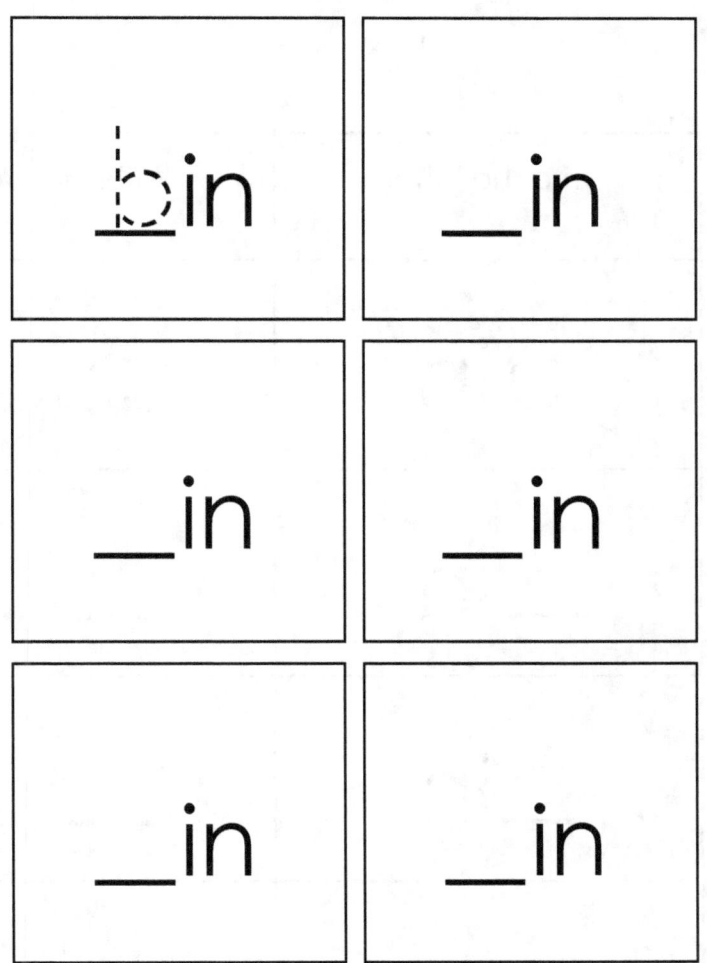

Teacher: Write these letters on the lines above.

b, d, f, p, t, w

Write words that end in "in"

Read the instructions, *below*, to the child. The child should do the sounding out and the writing.

Sound out ↓	Write the letter ↓	Write and read the word ↓
b	bin	b i n
f	_in	__ __ __
p	_in	__ __ __
t	_in	__ __ __
w	_in	__ __ __

Draw a line from the word to the picture

Say: "Read each word out loud. Then draw a line from the correct word to the picture."

sit
win
wit

fit
fin
kit

lit
pin
bit

pin
pit
fit

tin
win
wit

win
pit
pin

Play Bingo!

The Bingo game on the following pages reinforces short "i" words that end in "n" and "t." Cut out the flashcards on this page, grab a handful of pennies and you are all set to play.

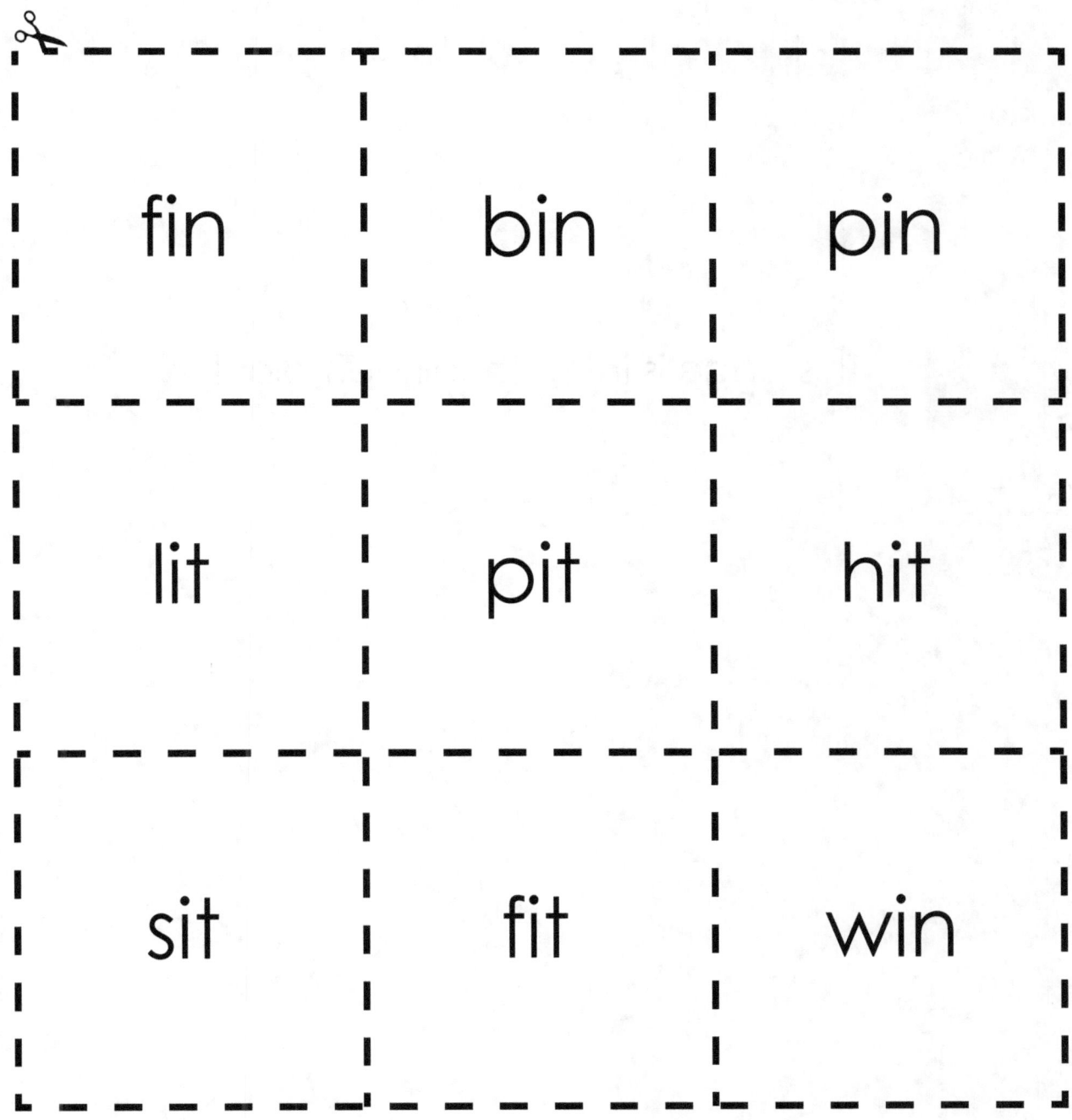

fin	bin	pin
lit	pit	hit
sit	fit	win

This page is intentionally left blank.

This page is intentionally left blank.

BINGO

sit	pit	fin
pin	hit	fit
win	bin	lit

BINGO

fin	bin	pin
lit	pit	hit
sit	fit	win

This page is intentionally left blank.

Make words that end in "p" and "g"

Sound out ↓	Write the letter ↓	Write and read the word ↓
r	_ip	_ _ _
d	_ig	_ _ _
d	_ip	_ _ _
w	_ig	_ _ _
z	_ip	_ _ _
b	_ig	_ _ _
s	_ip	_ _ _
p	_ig	_ _ _

Read more stories!

Instructions

Read a book

The child should read: "Jig and Mag." This is Book 7 in "Bob Books, Set 1."

Read online

1. Go to www.starfall.com.
2. Click on "Kindergarten" and then on the second item in the center (Language Arts) menu. It is called "Learn to Read."
3. Click on "The Big Hit" in the column that says, "Book." Make sure the computer's sound is on.
4. Tell the child to read the sentence that appears on the screen for each page. Don't let her click on the individual words because, if she does, the computer will read the words for her. You want the child to do all the reading. After she is done reading each sentence, she can click on the picture above it. The picture will then move in a delightful way.

Say: "**Read the words in each row out loud and circle the words in each row that are the same.**"

wag	wig	wag
fin	fan	fin
sat	sat	sit
tin	tan	tin
Dad	Dad	did
lid	lad	lid

Write the word and circle the picture

Say: "Read the word out loud. Then write it, and circle the picture that shows the word."

pan

___ ___ ___

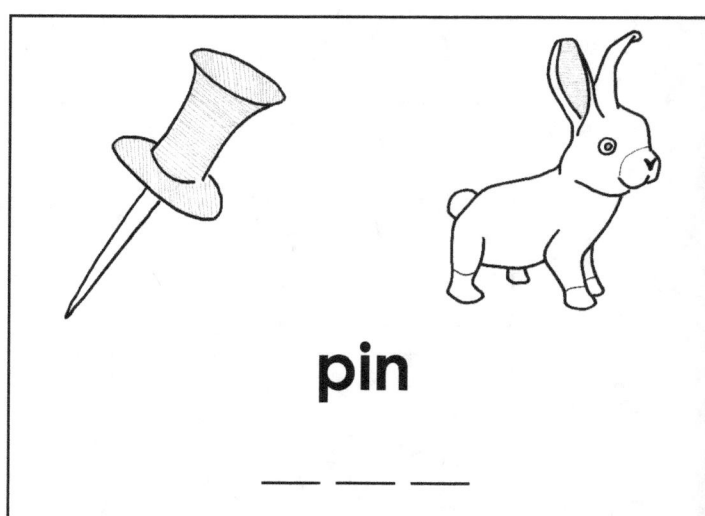

pin

___ ___ ___

fin

___ ___ ___

fan

___ ___ ___

sat

___ ___ ___

sit

___ ___ ___

Play Bingo!

This Bingo game reinforces short "i" words that end in various letters. Cut out the flashcards on this page and have fun! (The big X in the center of the gameboards that follow is a "free" space. Each of you can use that space on your boards to get five in a row.)

lid	hip	jam	win

pit	fat	bag	rat	had
can	pat	sit	kit	hat
mat	sat	pal	rip	hit
wig	gas	bat	bit	mat

This page is intentionally left blank.

This page is intentionally left blank.

BINGO

lid	hip	jam	win	bat
pit	fat	bag	rat	had
can	pat	✕	sit	kit
hat	mat	sat	pal	rip
hit	wig	gas	bit	mat

BINGO

pal	bit	gas	hit	hat
wig	mat	sat	fit	rip
kit	sit	✕	pat	can
pit	fat	bag	rat	had
bat	win	jam	hip	lid

This page is intentionally left blank.

Circle the letters

Say: **"Circle the correct letters. Then write the word."**

| d | z | a | i | g | p | d _ _ |

| c | b | i | a | f | t | _ _ _ |

| h | j | a | i | m | k | _ _ _ |

| p | m | i | a | g | n | _ _ _ |

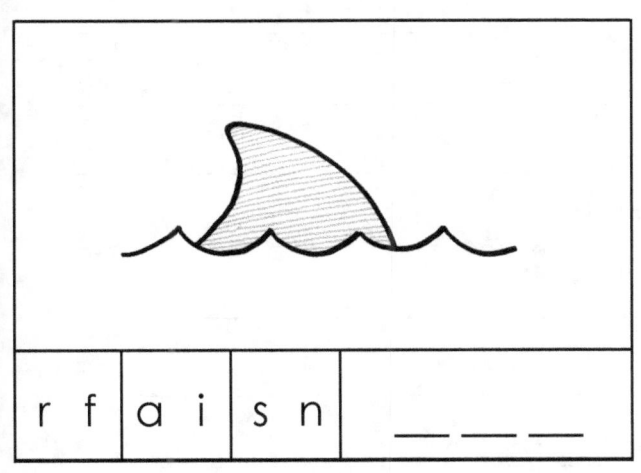

| r | f | a | i | s | n | _ _ _ |

| w | s | a | i | t | n | _ _ _ |

Does the sentence make sense?

Say: "In each of the following sentences, circle the word that will make the sentence make sense."

The tan cat was _____ .

fat   win

The pig is on the _____ .

zip   mat

The man was mad at _____ .

Dan   sit

The cat ran to the _____ .

man   sag

Sam did rip the _____ .

mat   wit

The cat hid in the _____ .

bag   dig

Short a and short i board game

First one to reach the end wins!

Instructions

<u>Materials you will need</u>: • A single die.
                                   • Coins to use as markers.
                                   • Gameboard, *opposite page.*

1. Each player places a coin on "start."
2. Take turns rolling the die.
3. Move forward the same amount of spaces as the number on the die.
4. As you move forward on the board, read the words that you pass, as well as the ones you land on.
5. For example, if a five comes up on the die, move five spaces on the game board and read five words.
6. The first person to reach the end wins the game.

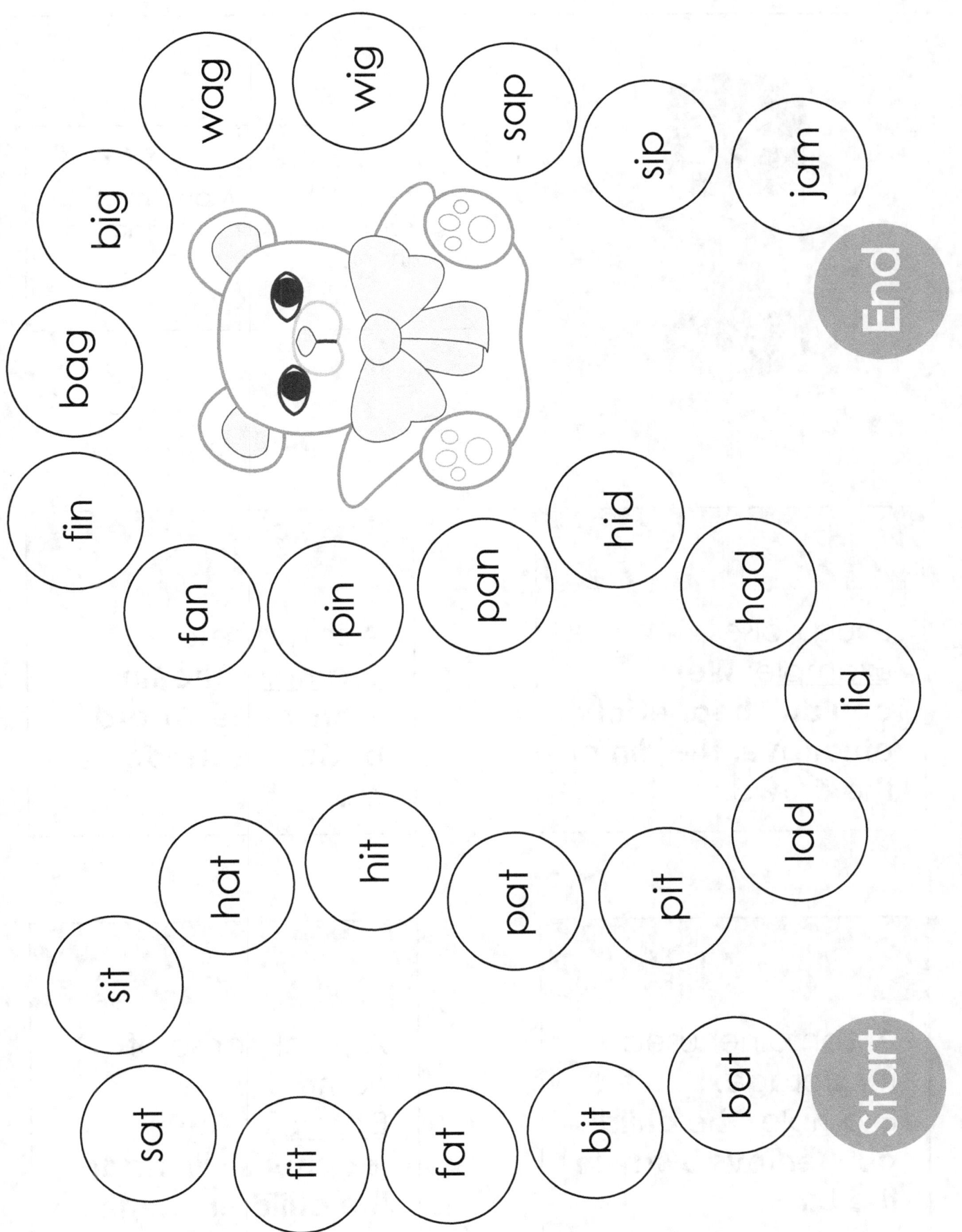

wag
wig
sap
sip
jam

big
bag
fin

End

fan
pin
pan
hid
had
lid
lad

sit
hat
hit
pat
pit

sat
fit
fat
bit
bat

Start

89

Read a book and learn new words

Read: "The Tin Man," by Barbara Makar, in "Primary Phonics, Set 1."

din

Loud noise.
Example: **We couldn't hear each other over the din of the crowd.**

tin

A shiny metal.
Example: **The Tin Man in The Wizard of Oz was made of tin.**

bin

A container used for storage.
Example: **The child put her toys away in the bin.**

wit

A quick sense of humor.
Example: **The teacher's wit made the children laugh.**

Instructions

1. Say: "**Now we're going to learn the sound** u **makes.** u **makes the /ŭ/ sound as in 'umbrella,' 'bug,' and 'fun.' Let's listen to it on the computer.**"

2. Go to www.starfall.com. Click on "Kindergarten," then "ABCs."

3. Click on the alphabet block for the letter u ." Every so often, as the child progresses through the activity, ask, "**What sound does** u **make?**"

4. The child should respond by making the short /ŭ/ sound.

5. After the child has done the u activity, click on the ⓤ circle at the bottom of the screen and listen to the song. When it is done, the website will ask you if you want to listen to the song again. Listen to the song as often as possible. Sing it when you are away from the computer too!

u says /ŭ/ as in

t u b

b u s

h u g

b u g

Instructions

Say: "**The letter** [u] **makes the /ŭ/ sound, as in 'bug.'**"
1. Have the child color in each picture and trace the letters below it.
2. Each time he or she finishes coloring in a picture, say, "**What sound does** [u] **make?**"
The child should make the /ŭ/ sound.
3. Each time he or she finishes tracing a word, say, "**What sound does** [u] **make?**" The
child should make the /ŭ/ sound.

93

Make words that end in "n" and "t"

Sound out ↓	Write the letter ↓	Write and read the word ↓
b	bun	b u n
n	_ut	__ __ __
f	_un	__ __ __
c	_ut	__ __ __
r	_un	__ __ __
b	_ut	__ __ __
s	_un	__ __ __

Write the word and circle the picture

Say: "Read the word out loud. Then write it, and circle the picture that shows the word."

run

— — —

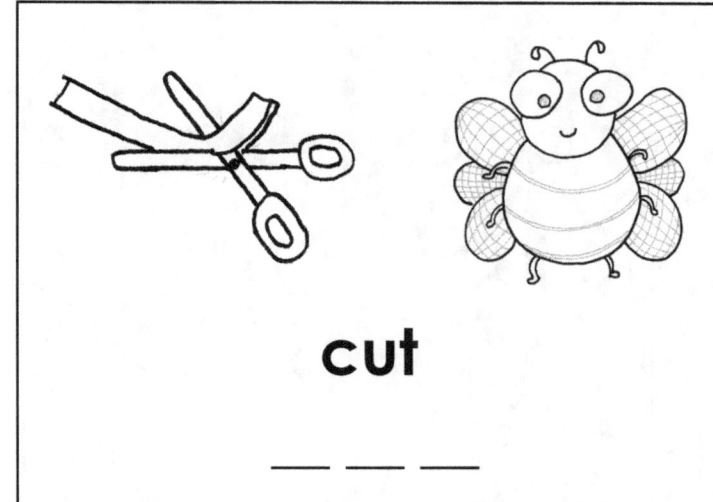

cut

— — —

bun

— — —

fun

— — —

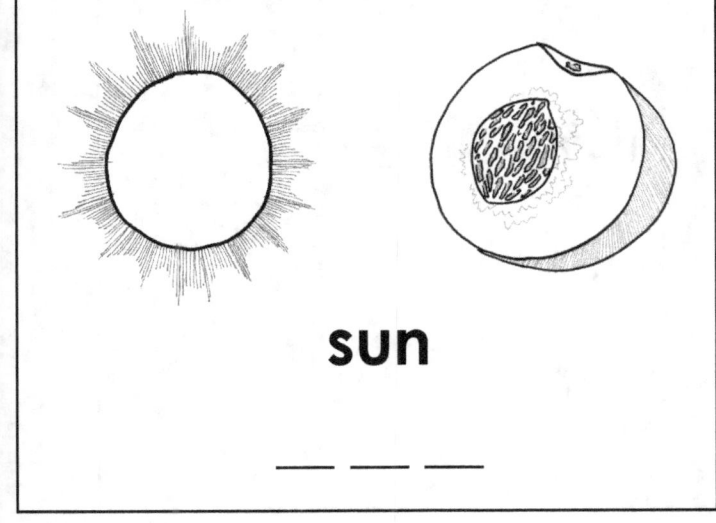

sun

— — —

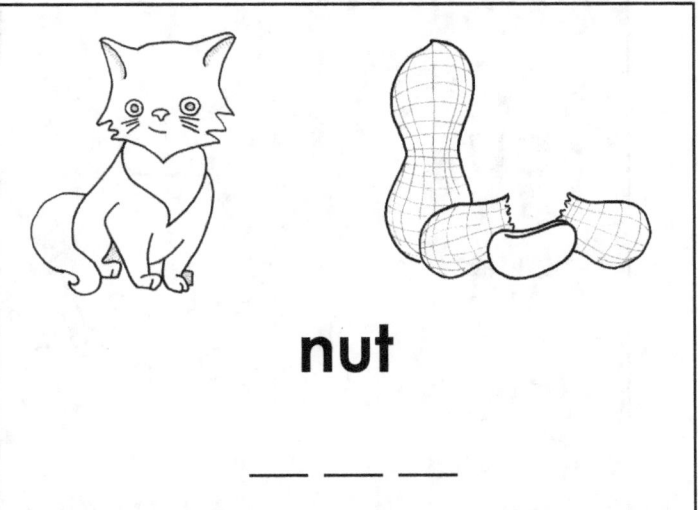

nut

— — —

Draw a line from the word to the picture

Say: "**Read each word out loud. Then draw a line from the correct word to the picture.**"

bun

nut

but

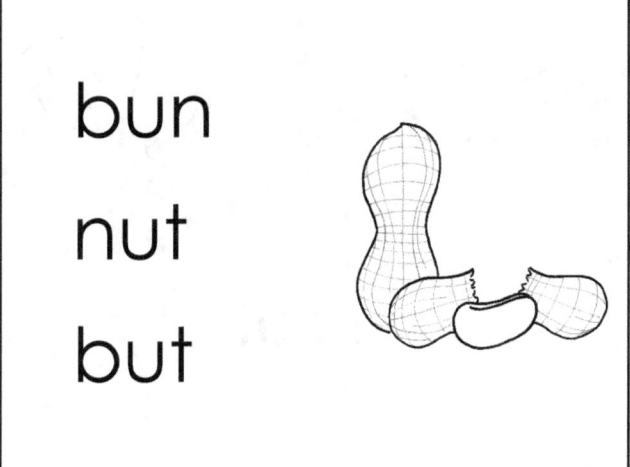

fun

hut

sun

fun

nut

run

but

cut

bun

cut

sun

but

nut

fun

bun

Words that end in "g," "p," or "s"

Sound out ↓	Write the letter ↓	Write and read the word ↓
b	bug	b u g
c	_up	___ ___ ___
h	_ug	___ ___ ___
b	_us	___ ___ ___
t	_ug	___ ___ ___
r	_ug	___ ___ ___
m	_ug	___ ___ ___

Draw a line from the word to the picture

Say: "Read each word out loud. Then draw a line from the correct word to the picture."

cup

bus

rug

pup

rug

bug

cup

dug

pup

bus

mug

hug

bus

tug

lug

cup

rug

bus

Write the word and circle the picture

Say: "**Read the word out loud. Then write it, and circle the picture that shows the word.**"

cup

— — —

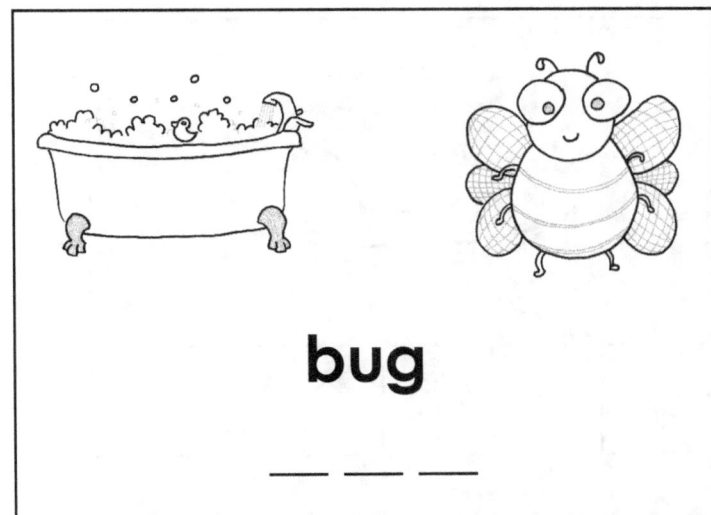

bug

— — —

rug

— — —

tug

— — —

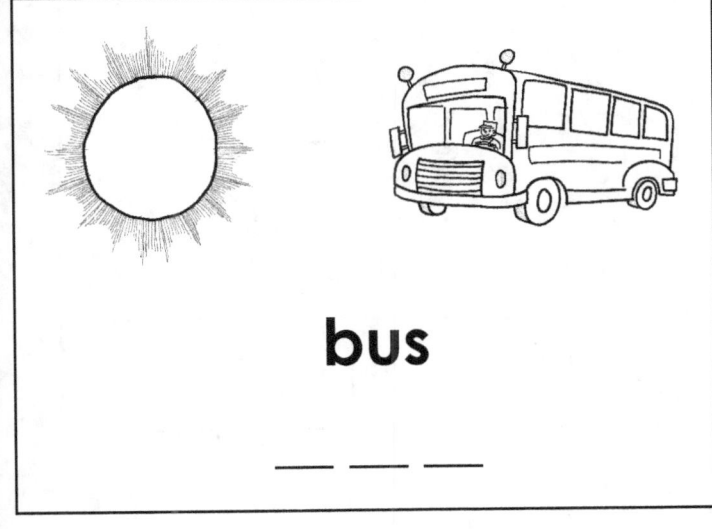

bus

— — —

dug

— — —

Circle the letters

Say: **"Circle the correct letters. Then write the word."**

| c | j | u | a | k | p | c u p |

| l | h | u | i | g | m | _ _ _ |

| h | b | i | u | s | f | _ _ _ |

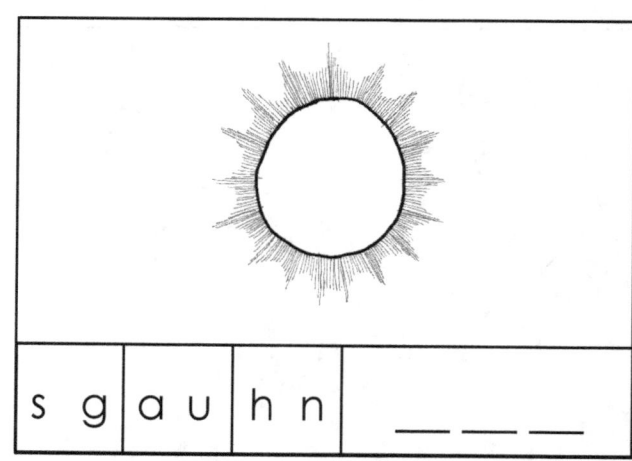

| s | g | a | u | h | n | _ _ _ |

| r | f | i | u | d | g | _ _ _ |

| p | b | u | i | p | c | _ _ _ |

What a difference one letter makes!

Say: "**Read the words in each row. Circle the words in each row that are the same.**"

bug	bun	bug

tub	tub	tug

run	rut	rut

rug	rug	run

but	but	bug

mud	mug	mud

Does the sentence make sense?

Say: "**When you read, it's important to ask yourself if what you just read makes sense. If a sentence makes sense, then you know you probably read it correctly.**" For each of the following sentences, circle the word that will make the sentence make sense.

The pup and Gus sit on the _____ .

bus   cup

It was fun in the _____ .

sun   rug

Sam has a _____ for Mat.

bag   dug

Mat had a nut in a _____ .

cup   tug

Gus and _____ hug.

Pam   bug

Play Bingo!

The Bingo game on the following pages reinforces short "u" words. Cut out the flashcards on this page, grab a handful of pennies and you are all set to play.

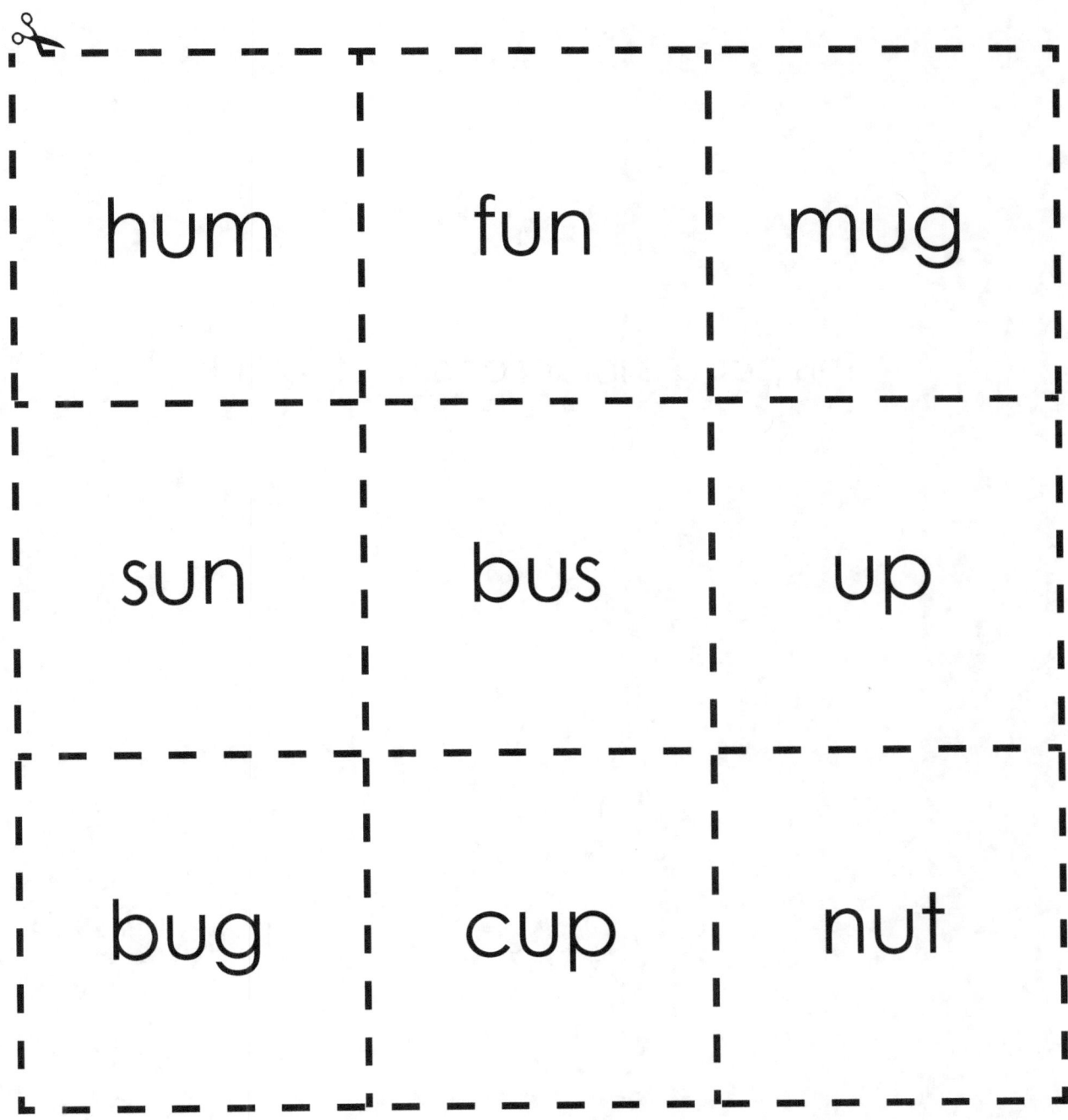

hum	fun	mug
sun	bus	up
bug	cup	nut

This page is intentionally left blank.

This page is intentionally left blank.

BINGO

mug	cup	hum
fun	nut	sun
bug	up	bus

BINGO

hum	fun	mug
sun	bus	up
bug	cup	nut

This page is intentionally left blank.

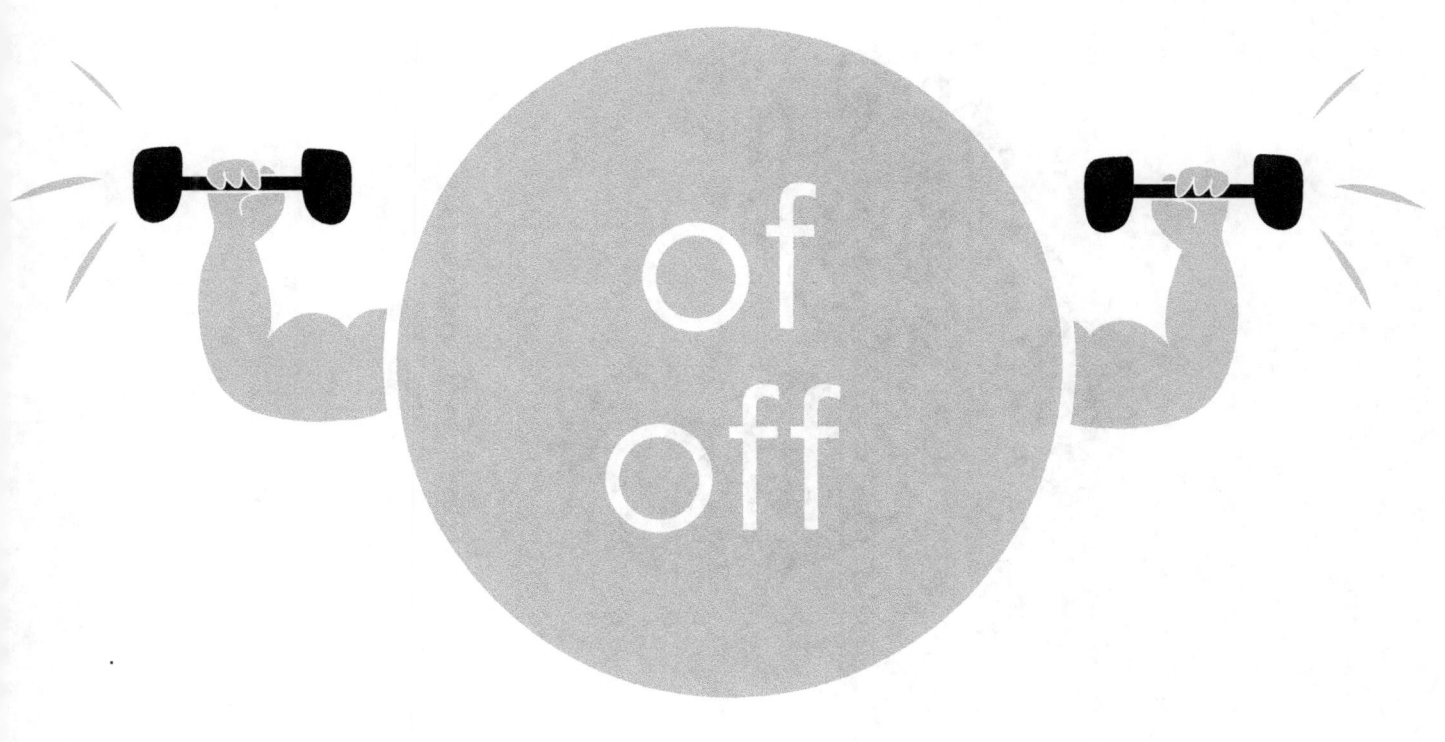

Read more stories!

Instructions

Read a book

The child should read: "Muff and Ruff." This is Book 8 in Bob Books Set 1.

Read online

1. Go to www.starfall.com.
2. Click on "Kindergarten" and then on the second item in the center (Language Arts) menu. It is called "Learn to Read."
3. Click on "Gus the Duck" in the column that says, "Book." Make sure the computer's sound is on.
4. Tell the child to read the sentence that appears on the screen for each page. Don't let her click on the individual words because, if she does, the computer will read the words for her. You want the child to do all the reading. After she is done reading each sentence, she can click on the picture above it. The picture will then move in a delightful way.

Say: "Look at how changing the middle vowel changes the word!
Read all the words out loud and draw a line from the correct word to the picture."

tab
tub

tag
tug

cap
cup

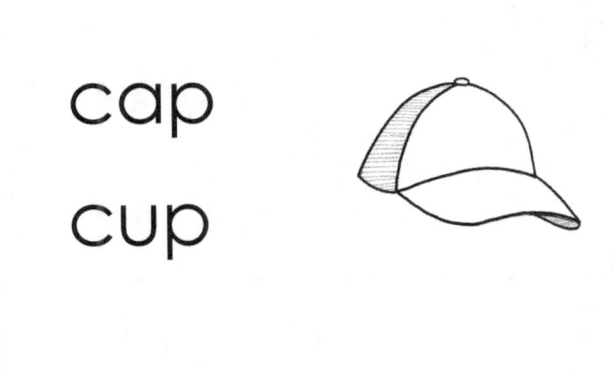

rag
rug

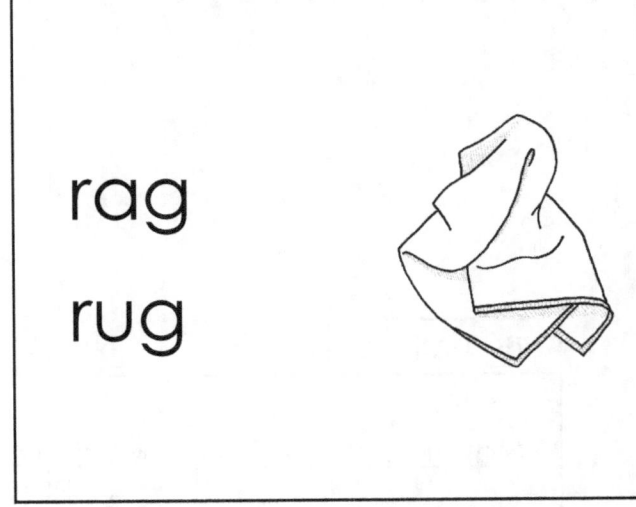

bag
big
bug

ban
bin
bun

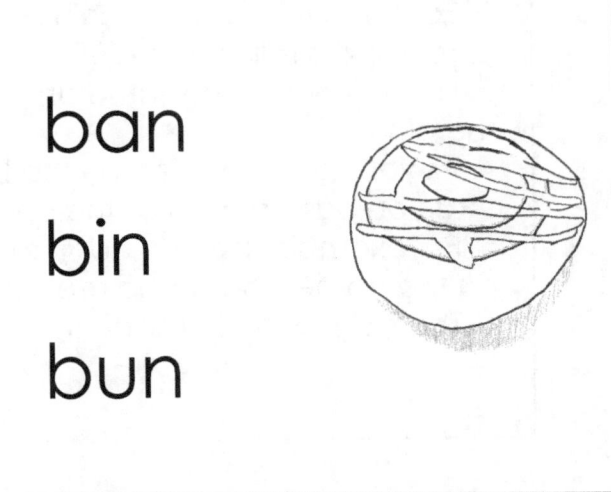

Play the short a, i, and u board game

First one to reach the end wins!

Instructions

<u>Materials you will need</u>:
- A single die.
- Coins to use as markers.
- Gameboard, *opposite page*.

1. Each player places a coin on "start."
2. Take turns rolling the die.
3. Move forward the same amount of spaces as the number on the die.
4. As you move forward on the board, make read the words that you pass, as well as the ones you land on.
5. For example, if a five comes up on the die, move five spaces on the game board and read five words.
6. The first person to reach the end wins the game.

pat · pit · bag · big · bug

hut · rat · rib

hit · rut · tug · rub

hat · lad · tag · ram

sit · lid · fun · run

sat · ham · fin · End

but · him · fan

bit · hum · tug

bat · tag

Start

This page is intentionally left blank.

rut

1. A long ditch at the side of a dirt road.
2. A habit.
Example: **She was stuck in a rut.**

lug

To carry something heavy.
Example: **She will lug a stack of books up the stairs.**

hut

A small, simple house.
Example: **The villagers live in huts.**

pug

A small dog with a flat nose and wrinkled face.
Example: **The pug barked.**

bud

An undeveloped leaf or flower.
Example: **The bud on the tree will soon be a flower.**

Read more stories!

Instructions

Read a book

The child should read: "Tim" in Primary Phonics, Set 1.

This book is great for short /u/ practice but it has some short /o/ words in it too. Point these words out to the child and tell him he will learn the sound of /o/ soon but that, for now, you will read the short /o/ words whenever they come up. Don't ask the child to read them. For now, focus exclusively on the short /a/, /i/, and /u/ words.

Instructions

1. Say: "**Now we're going to learn the sound [e] makes. [e] makes the /ĕ/ sound as in 'elephant,' 'pet,' and 'get.' Let's listen to it on the computer.**"

2. Go to www.starfall.com. Click on "Kindergarten," then "ABCs.""

3. Click on the alphabet block for the letter [e]. Every so often, as the child progresses through the activity, ask, "**What sound does [e] make?**"

4. The child should respond by making the short /ĕ/ sound.

5. After the child has done the [e] activity, click on the (e) circle at the bottom of the screen and listen to the song. When it is done, the website will ask you if you want to listen to the song again. Listen to the song as often as possible. Sing it when you are away from the computer too!

e says /ĕ/ as in

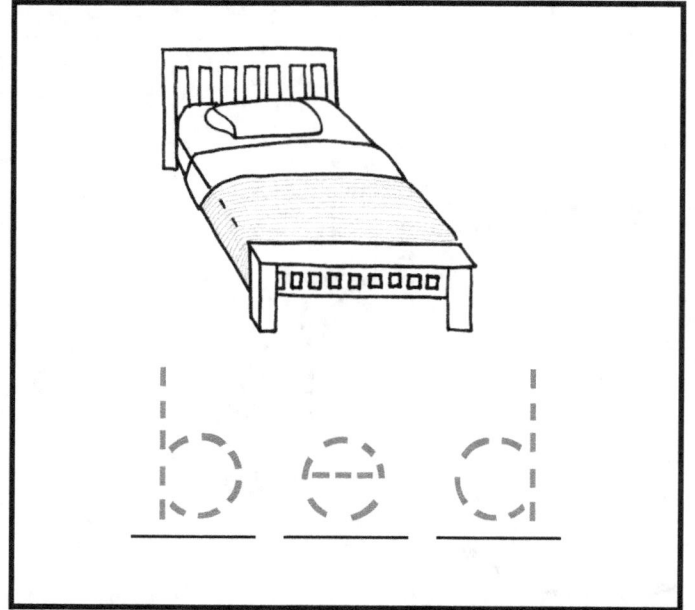

b e d

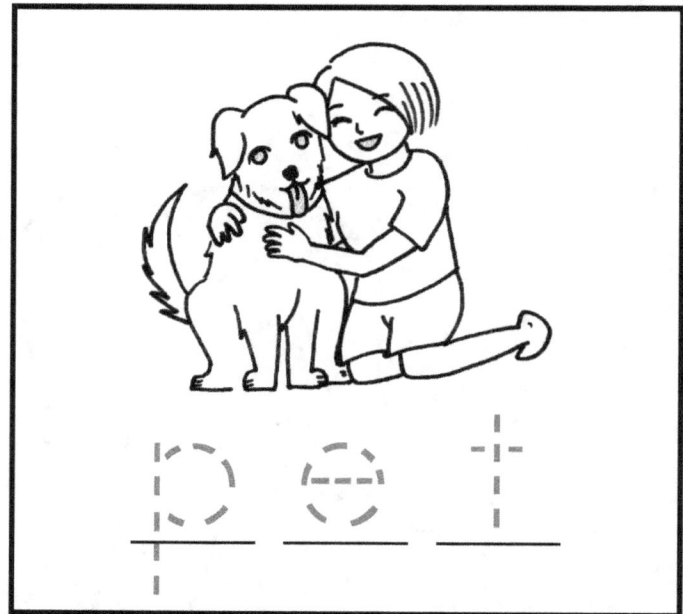

p e t

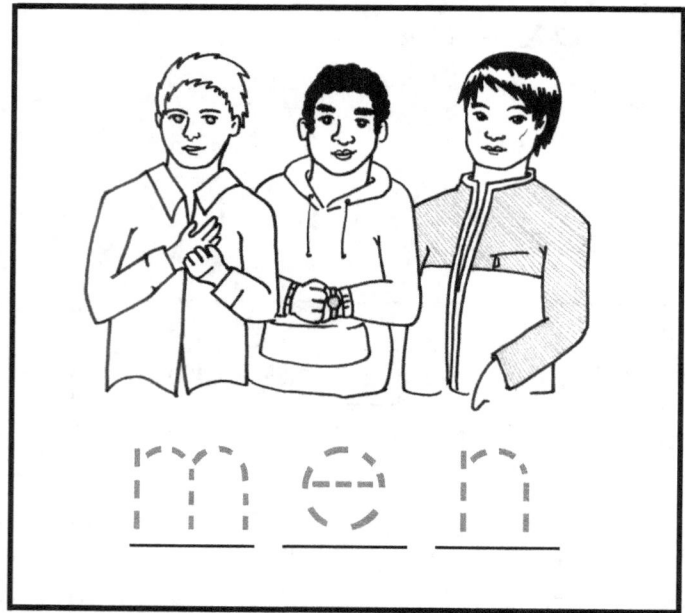

m e n

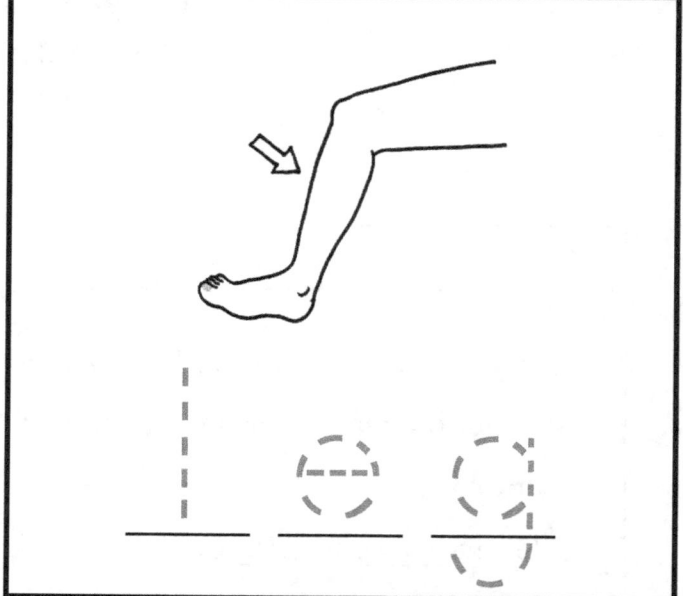

l e g

Instructions

Say: "**The letter** [e] **makes the /ĕ/ sound, as in egg.**"

1. Have the child color in each picture and trace the words below it.

2. Each time he or she finishes coloring in a picture, say, "**What sound does** [e] **make?**" The child should make the /ĕ/ sound.

3. Each time he or she finishes tracing a word, say, "**What sound does** [e] **make?**" The child should make the /ĕ/ sound.

Write and read the word

Sound out ↓	Write the letter ↓	Write and read the word ↓
b	bet	b e t
w	_et	_ _ _
n	_et	_ _ _
p	_et	_ _ _
g	_et	_ _ _
j	_et	_ _ _
m	_et	_ _ _

Write the word and circle the picture

Say: "Read the word out loud. Write the word. Circle the picture that shows the word."

wet

— — —

pet

— — —

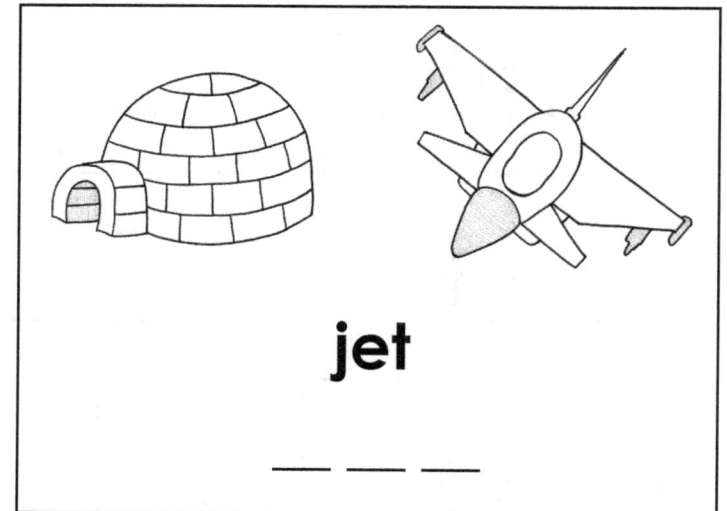

jet

— — —

net

— — —

met

— — —

Draw a line from the word to the picture

Say: **"Read each word. Then draw a line from the correct word to the picture."**

wet

pet

get

wet

bet

jet

met

let

set

let

wet

net

net

jet

pet

met

get

jet

Words that end in "n," "d," or "g"

Sound out ↓	Write the letter ↓	Write and read the word ↓
h	hen	h e n
b	_ed	_ _ _ _
m	_en	_ _ _ _
l	_eg	_ _ _ _
p	_en	_ _ _ _
r	_ed	_ _ _ _
t	_en	_ _ _ _

Write the word and circle the picture

Say: "Read the word out loud. Write it and circle the picture that shows the word."

wet

___ ___ ___

pet

___ ___ ___

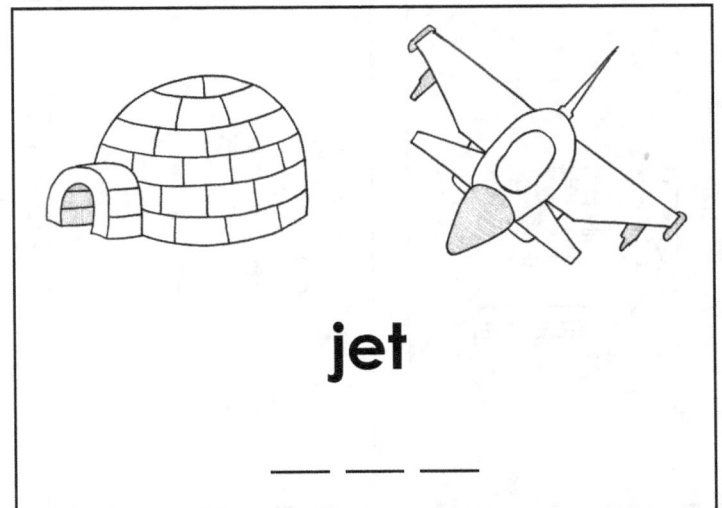

jet

___ ___ ___

net

___ ___ ___

met

___ ___ ___

Draw a line from the word to the picture

Say: "**Read each word out loud. Then draw a line from the correct word to the picture.**"

wet

hen

pen

red

ten

wed

bet

bed

men

ten

den

pet

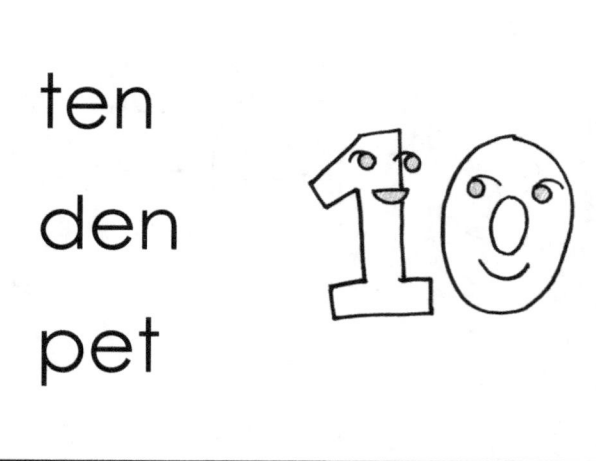

met

Ben

leg

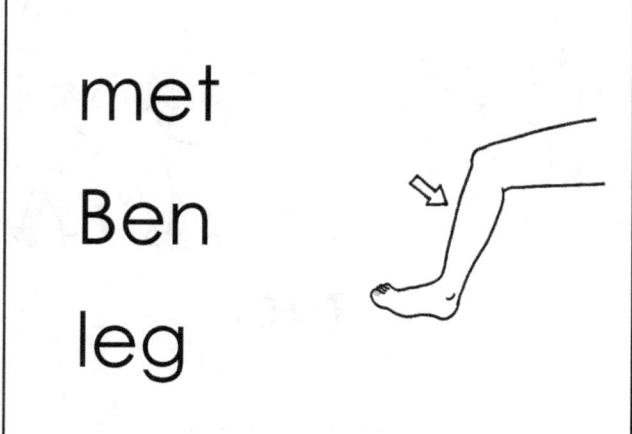

get

jet

hen

What a difference one letter makes!

Say: "**Read the words in each row out loud and circle the words that are the same.**"

pet	peg	pet

web	web	wet

beg	bet	beg

men	men	met

let	let	leg

pen	pet	pen

wet	wed	wet

Does the sentence make sense?

Say: "**When you read, it's important to ask yourself if what you just read makes sense. If a sentence makes sense, then you know you probably read it correctly.**" For each of the following sentences, circle the word that will make the sentence make sense.

Ten men sat on the _____ .

rug   pan

The pan is in the _____ .

bag   beg

Ed can run to the _____ .

bed   sat

Ken and Ben _____ .

met   ham

The pet is _____ .

wet   sip

Play Bingo!

This Bingo game reinforces short "e" words that end in various letters. Cut out the flashcards on this page and have fun! (The big X in the gameboards that follow is a "free" space. Each of you can use that space on your boards to get five in a row.)

hen	leg	wet	bed

end	den	beg	let	men
jet	set	egg	Ben	exit
red	peg	ten	pen	pep
ten	net	Ed	fed	get

This page is intentionally left blank.

This page is intentionally left blank.

BINGO

egg	hen	leg	wet	bed
end	den	beg	let	men
jet	set	✕	Ben	exit
red	peg	pet	pen	pep
ten	net	Ed	fed	get

BINGO

bed	den	men	peg	exit
ten	egg	leg	jet	beg
Ben	pep	✕	hen	pet
Ed	pen	red	end	wet
net	let	fed	set	get

This page is intentionally left blank.

Instructions

Read a book

The child should read:
- "Peg and Ted." This is Book 10 in Bob Books Set 1.
- "The Vet." This is Book 12 in Bob Books, Set 1.

Read online

1. Go to www.starfall.com.
2. Click "Kindergarten" and then on the second item in the center (Language Arts) menu. It is called "Learn to Read."
3. Click on "Peg and Hen" in the column that says, "Book." Make sure the computer's sound is on.
4. Tell the child to read the sentence that appears on the screen for each page. Don't let her click on the individual words because, if she does, the computer will read the words for her. You want the child to do all the reading. After she is done reading each sentence, she can click on the picture above it. The picture will then move in a delightful way.

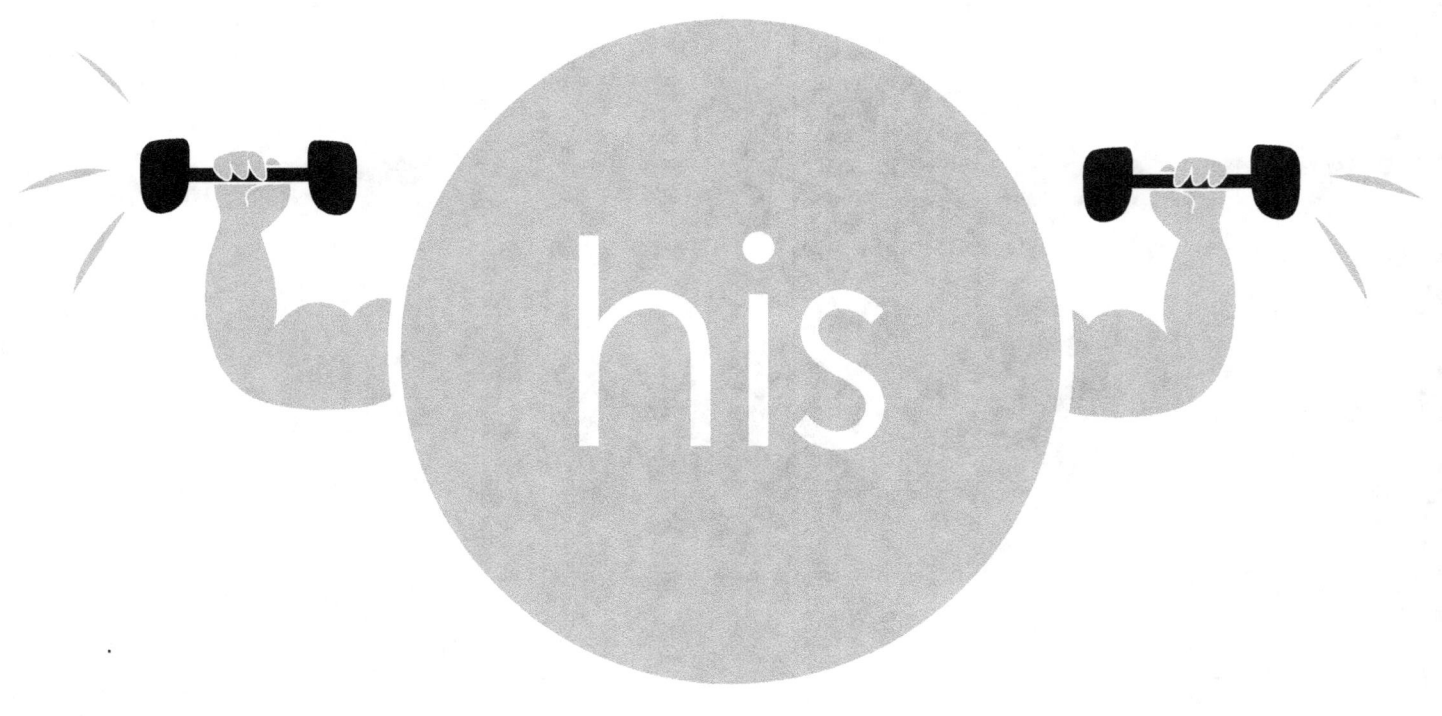

his

his

his

his

Say: "**Look at how changing the middle vowel changes the word! Read each word out loud.**"

bet	bat	but
pet	pat	pit
bet	bit	but
set	sit	sat
pen	pin	pan
ten	tin	tan
bed	bad	bid
beg	big	bug
peg	pig	pug

Play the short a, i, u, and e board game

First one to reach the end wins!

Instructions

<u>Materials you will need</u>:
- A single die.
- Coins to use as markers.
- Gameboard, *opposite page*.

1. Each player places a coin on "start."
2. Take turns rolling the die.
3. Move forward the same amount of spaces as the number on the die.
4. As you move forward on the board, read the words that you pass, as well as the ones you land on.
5. For example, if a five comes up on the die, move five spaces on the game board and read five words.
6. The first person to reach the end wins the game.

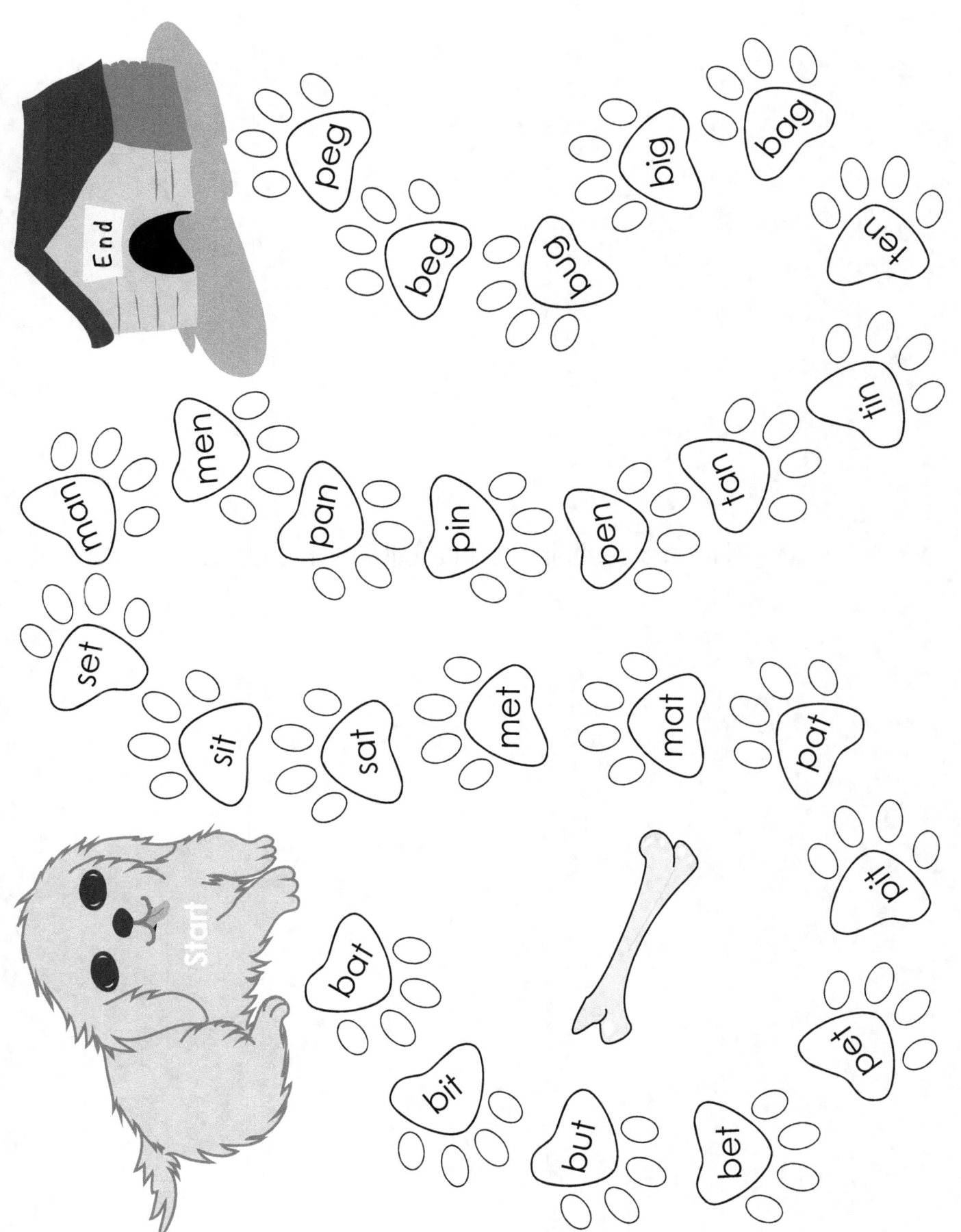

This page is intentionally left blank.

Read a book and learn new words

The child should read: "The Jet" in Primary Phonics, Set 1.

pep

Energy.
<u>Example</u>: **She still had a lot of pep, even though it was time to go to sleep.**

den

A room in a house used for working, reading, or watching TV.

hen

A female chicken.

Say: **"Many kids have a hard time telling 'b' and 'd' apart. Here is a fun way to remember! It's called the bed trick.**

"The word 'bed' starts with 'b' and ends with 'd.'"

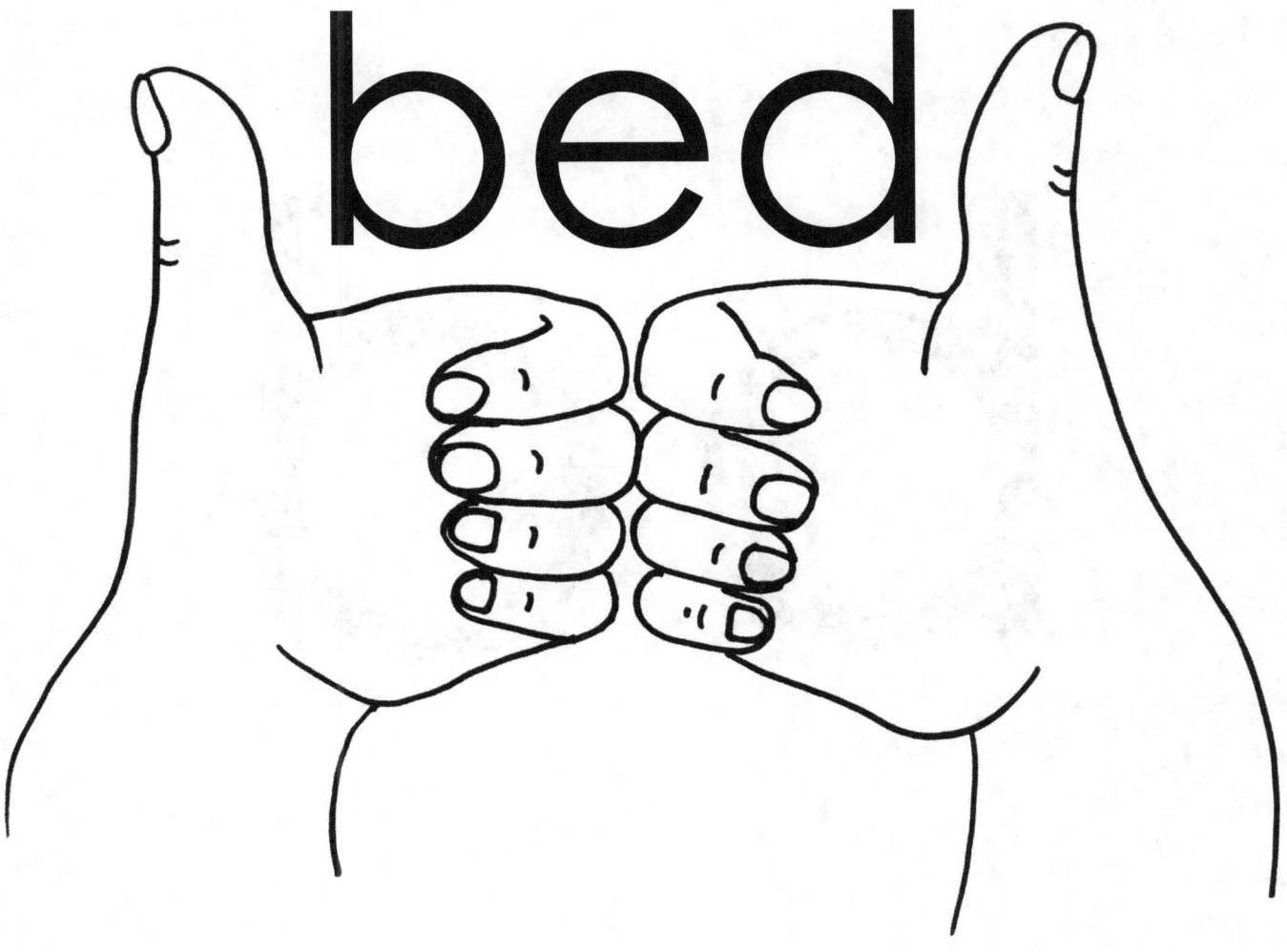

Say: "**Make a 'bed' with your two hands, as shown in the picture above, and imagine the word 'bed' between your fingers.**" (Turn the page →)

The Bed Trick

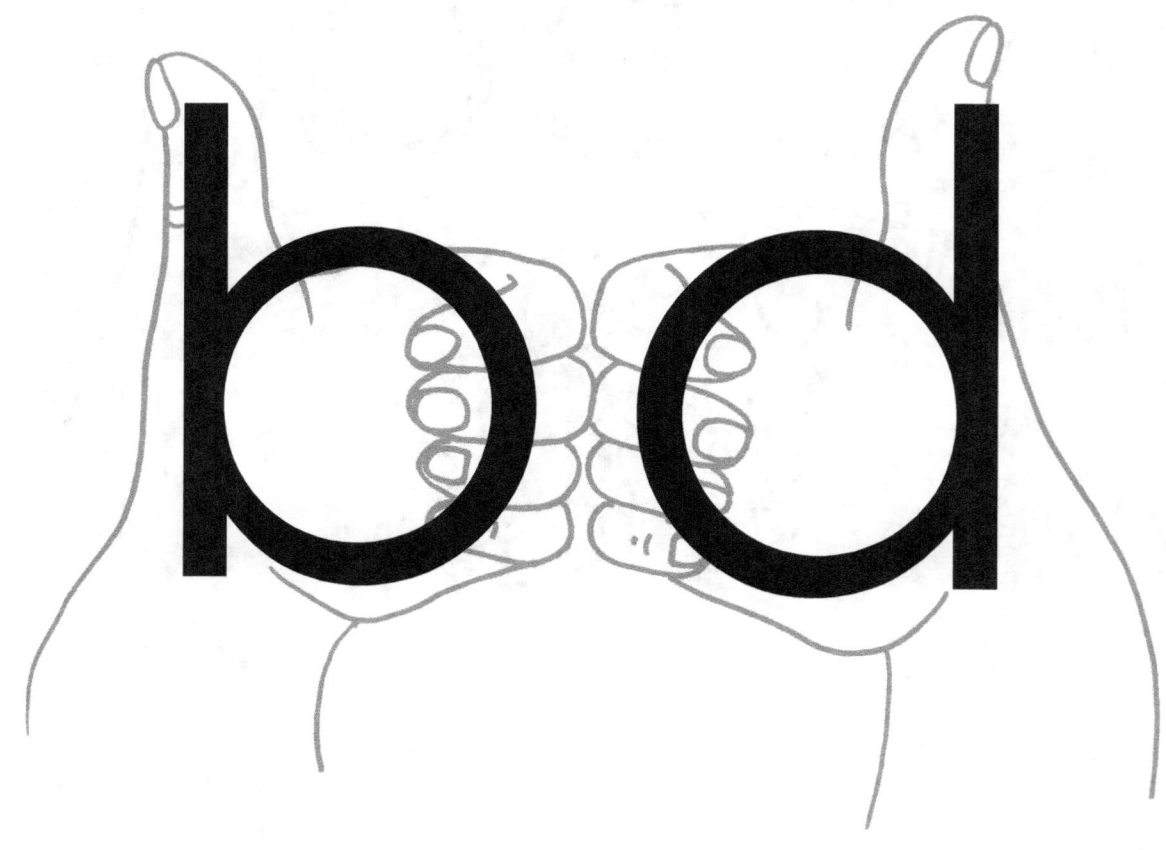

Say: "**Any time you are not sure if a word has a 'b' or a 'd' in it, hold your hands in the bed trick position and match the letter you are trying to figure out to the correct hand.**'"

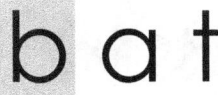

Is the first letter b or d?

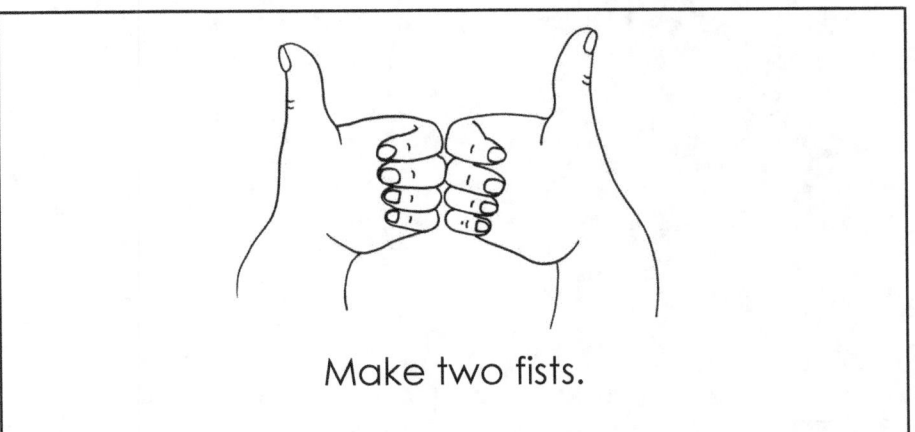

Make two fists.

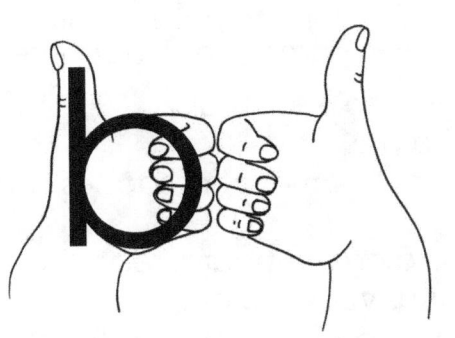

The letter looks like the first fist, so it is b.

Play the "b or d" board game

Use the bed trick as you play!

Instructions

<u>Materials you will need</u>: • A single die.
• Coins to use as markers.
• Gameboard, *opposite page*.

1. Each player places a coin on "start."
2. Take turns rolling the die.
3. Move forward the same amount of spaces as the number on the die.
4. As you move forward on the board, read the words that you pass, as well as the ones you land on.
5. For example, if a five comes up on the die, move five spaces on the game board and read five words.
6. The first person to reach the end wins the game.

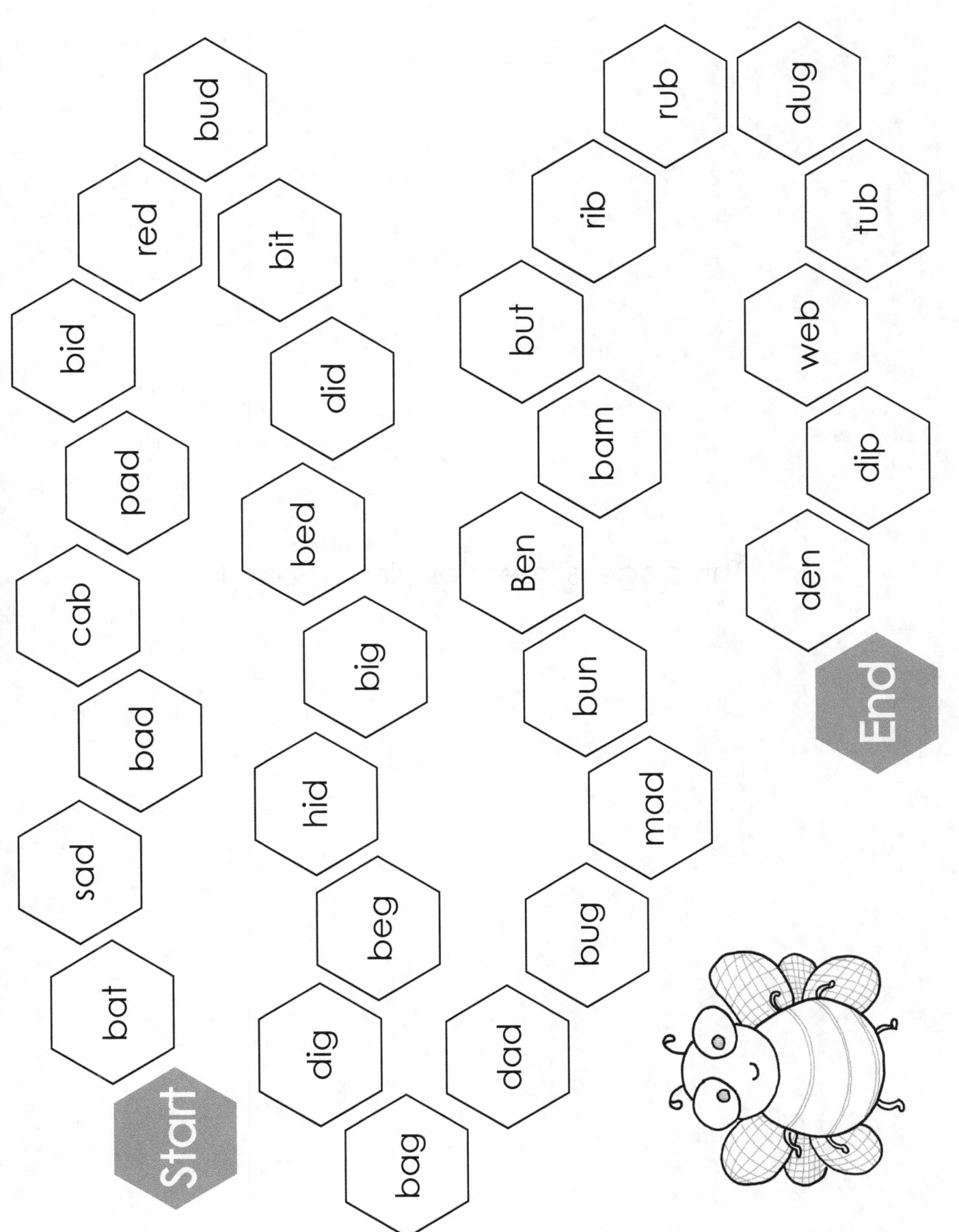

bud

red

bit

bid

did

pad

bed

cab

big

bad

hid

sad

beg

bat

dig

Start

bag

dad

bug

mad

bun

Ben

bam

but

rib

rub

dug

tub

web

dip

den

End

145

This page is intentionally left blank.

Instructions

1. Say: "**Now we're going to learn the sound** o **makes.** o **makes the** /ŏ/ **sound as in 'octopus,' 'hop' and 'top.' Let's listen to it on the computer.**"

2. Go to www.starfall.com. Click on "Kindergarten," then "ABCs.""

3. Click on the alphabet block for the letter o . Every so often, as the child progresses through the activity, ask, "**What sound does** o **make?**"

4. The child should respond by making the short /ŏ/ sound.

5. After the child has done the o activity, click on the ⊙ circle at the bottom of the screen and listen to the song. When it is done, the website will ask you if you want to listen to the song again. Listen to the song as often as possible. Sing it when you are away from the computer too!

o says /ŏ/ as in

h o p

c o p

m o m

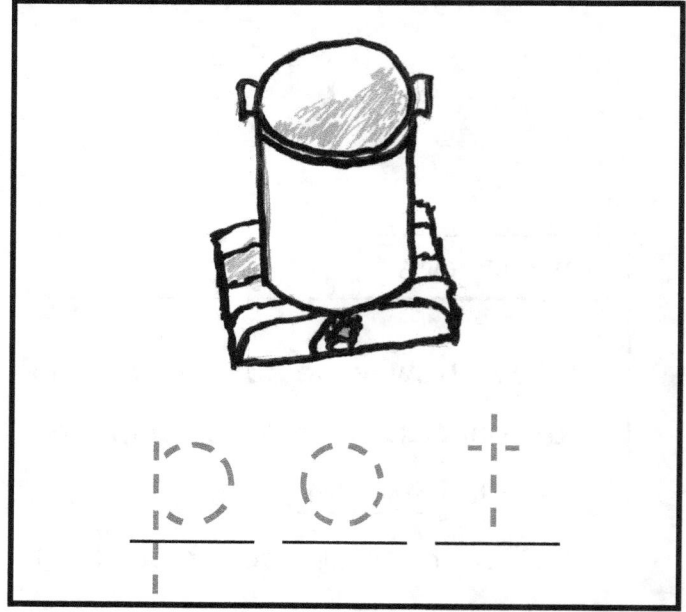

p o t

Instructions

Say: "**The letter** o **makes the /ŏ/ sound, as in 'octopus.'**"
1. Have the child color in each picture and trace the letters below it.
2. Each time he or she finishes coloring in a picture, say, "**What sound does** o **make?**"
The child should make the /ŏ/ sound.
3. Each time he or she finishes tracing a set of three letters, say, "**What sound does** o
make?" The child should make the /ŏ/ sound.

Write and read the word

Sound out ↓	Write the letter ↓	Write and read the word ↓
h	hot	hot
n	_ot	___
c	_ot	___
g	_ot	____
p	_ot	___
t	_ot	____
r	_ot	___

Write the word and circle the picture

Say: "**Read the word out loud. Then write the word, and circle the picture that shows the word.**"

hot

___ ___ ___

tot

___ ___ ___

jot

___ ___ ___

pot

___ ___ ___

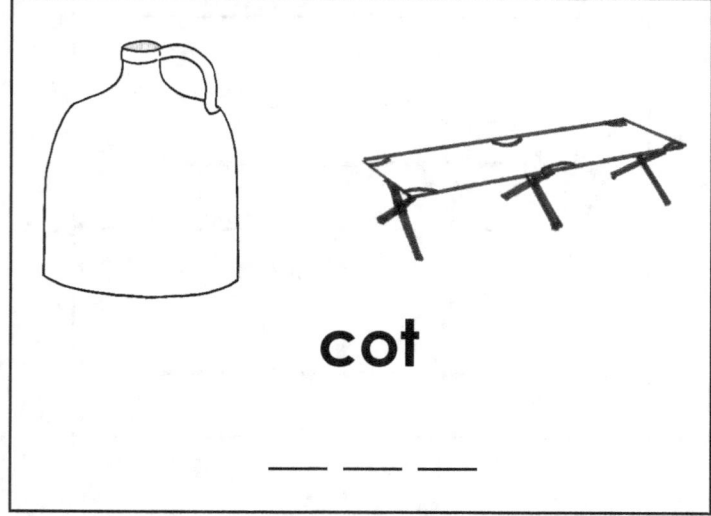

cot

___ ___ ___

rot

___ ___ ___

Draw a line from the word to the picture

Say: "**Read each word out loud. Then draw a line from the correct word to the picture.**"

pot
hot

cot
hot

not
hot

got
tot

got
jot

rot
not

Sound out ↓	Write the letter ↓	Write and read the word ↓
h	hop	h o p
m	_om	— — — —
c	_op	— — — —
h	_og	— — — —
m	_op	— — — —
j	_og	— — — —
t	_op	— — — —

Write the word and circle the picture

Say: "Read the word out loud. Then write it, and circle the picture that shows the word."

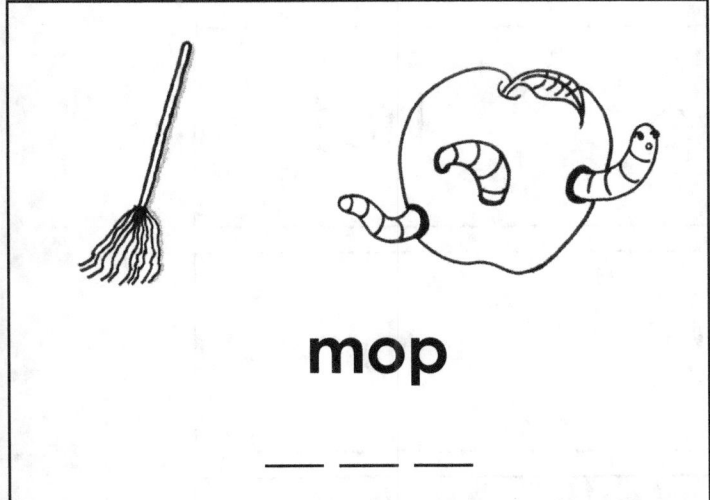

mop

— — —

hop

— — —

mom

— — —

hog

— — —

jog

— — —

cop

— — —

What a difference one letter makes!

Say: "Read the words in each row out loud. Circle the words in each row that are the same."

hot	hop	hot
mop	top	top
cot	cot	cop
pop	pot	pop
got	dot	got
job	sob	sob
fog	jog	fog

Draw a line from the word to the picture

Say: "Read each word out loud. Then draw a line from the correct word to the picture."

mom
hop
top

cop
mop
mom

jog
hop
hog

mop
top
mom

mop
jog
mom

hog
hop
top

Circle the letters

Say: **"Circle the correct letters. Then write the word."**

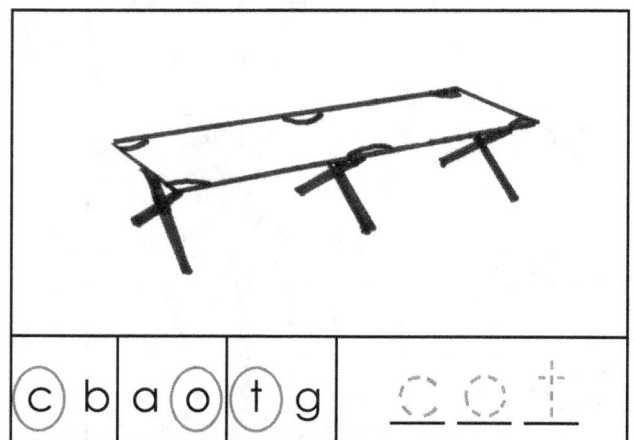

c	b	a	o	t	g	c o t

n	m	o	i	m	j	_ _ _ _

f	p	o	e	h	t	_ _ _ _

h	k	u	o	g	l	_ _ _ _

n	j	o	i	g	m	_ _ _ _

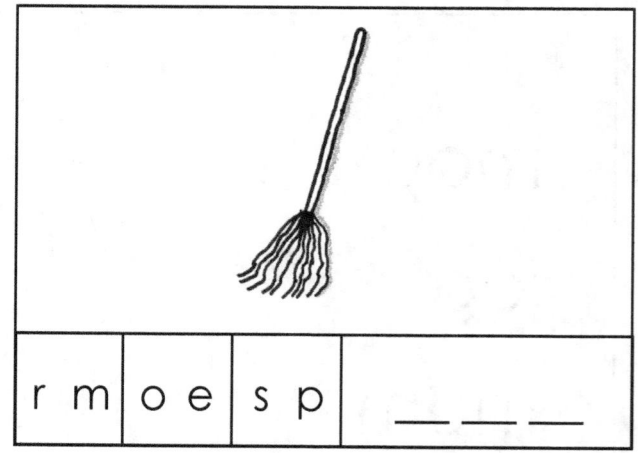

r	m	o	e	s	p	_ _ _ _

Play Bingo!

The Bingo game on the following pages reinforces short "o" words. Cut out the flashcards on this page, grab a handful of pennies and you are all set to play.

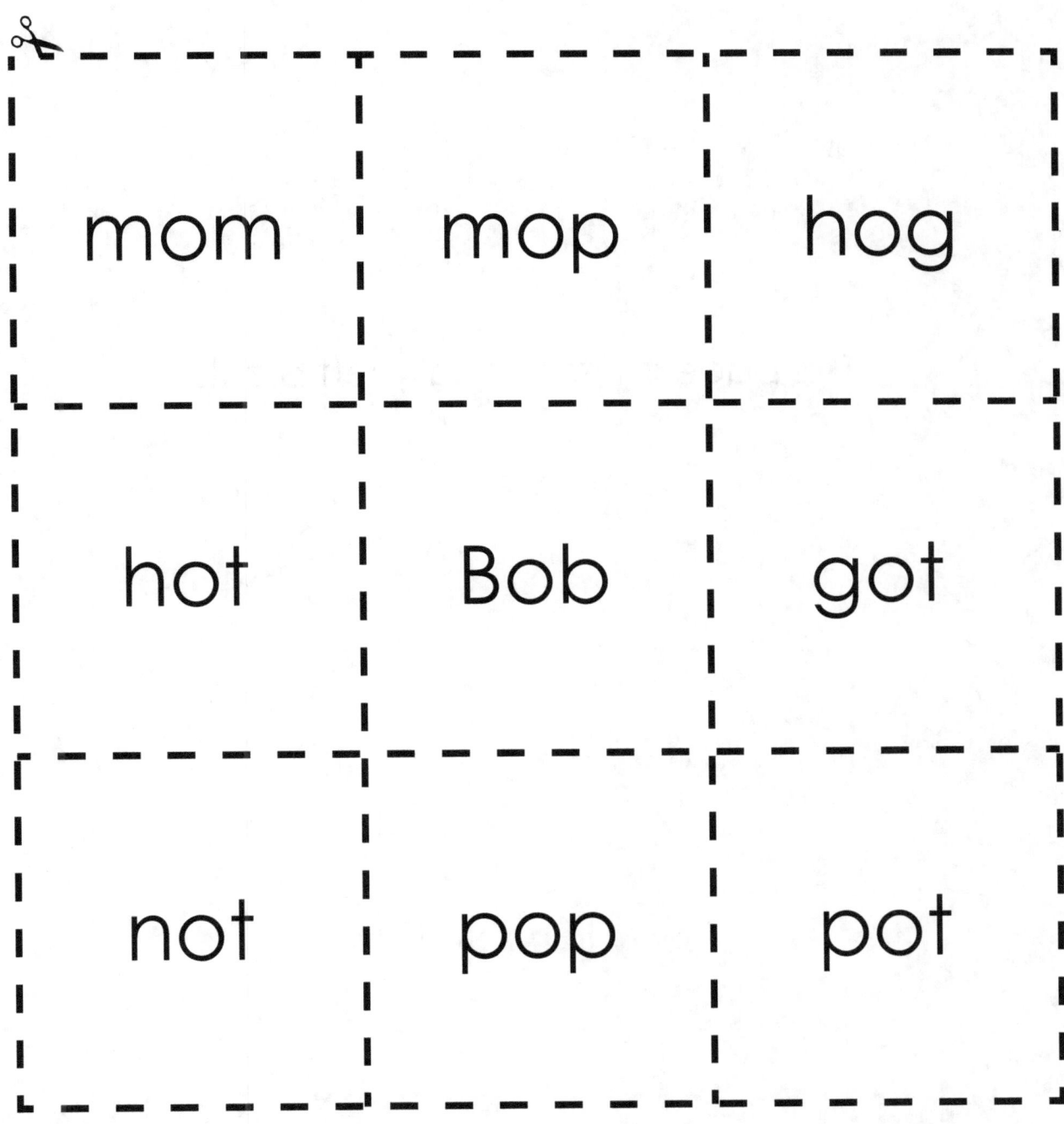

mom	mop	hog
hot	Bob	got
not	pop	pot

This page is intentionally left blank.

This page is intentionally left blank.

BINGO

mom	mop	hog
hot	Bob	got
not	pop	pot

BINGO

not	got	Bob
hot	mom	hog
pop	pot	mop

This page is intentionally left blank.

Say: "Sometimes, even though they look like they should follow a rule, some words are pronounced differently than words that have the same middle vowel and ending letter. 'Dog' is a great example of this. The word 'dog' is pronounced differently than 'hog,' 'fog,' and 'jog.' Because it doesn't follow any rules, we will add it to our list of words that need to be memorized."

dog

dog

dog

dog

Does the sentence make sense?

Say: "**When you read, it's important to ask yourself if what you just read makes sense. If a sentence makes sense, then you know you probably read it correctly.**" For each of the following sentences, circle the word that will make the sentence make sense.

The men pet the _____ .

pan   cat

Ed had a hot bun in the _____ .

pan   pin

A man had a big bag on the _____ .

hot   bus

The hog sat on the _____ .

rug   men

Ben had a nap in his _____ .

bed   bug

Instructions

Read a book

Bob Books, Set 1, has 4 good books to read for short o. These are:

- "Dot," Book 3
- "Mac," Book 4
- "Dot and Mit," Book 5
- "Dot and the Dog," Book 6

Read online

1. Go to www.starfall.com.
2. Click on "Kindergarten" and then on the second item in the center (Language Arts) menu. It is called "Learn to Read."
3. Click on "Mox's Shop" in the column that says, "Book." Make sure the computer's sound is on.
4. Tell the child to read the sentence that appears on the screen for each page. Don't let her click on the individual words because, if she does, the computer will read the words for her. You want the child to do all the reading. After she is done reading each sentence, she can click on the picture above it. The picture will then move in a delightful way.

for

for

for

for

Review: Short a, i, u, e, o

Say: **"Look at how changing the vowel changes the word! Read each word out loud."**

cop	cap	cup
top	tap	tip
hot	hat	hit
cot	cat	cut
pot	pit	pet
rot	rat	rut

Play the short vowel review board game

First one to reach the end wins!

Instructions

<u>Materials you will need</u>: • A single die.
• Coins to use as markers.
• Gameboard, *opposite page.*

1. Each player places a coin on "start."
2. Take turns rolling the die.
3. Move forward the same amount of spaces as the number on the die.
4. As you move forward on the board, read the words that you pass, as well as the ones you land on.
5. For example, if a five comes up on the die, move five spaces on the game board and read five words.
6. The first person to reach the end wins the game.

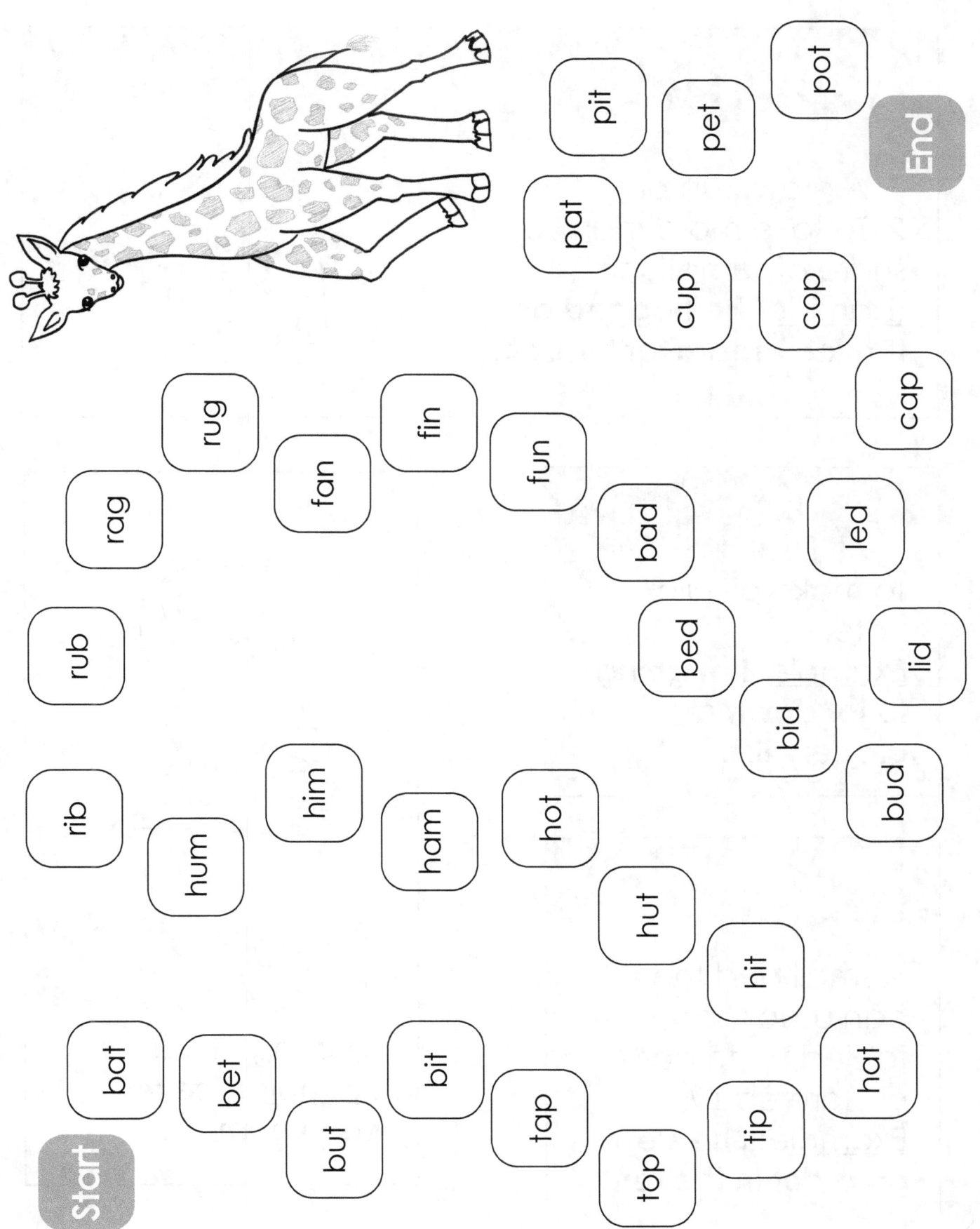

Start

bat bet but bit tap top tip hat hit hut hot ham him hum rib rub rag rug fan fin fun bad bed bid bud lid led cap cop cup pat pet pit pot

End

169

Vocabulary

hog

1. A grown up pig.
2. To take more than your share of something
Example: **He hogged all the ice cream for himself.**

jot

To make a quick note.
Example: **I'm going to jot down a grocery list.**

cot

A small bed that can usually be folded up to carry or store easily.
Example: **She slept on a cot in the tent.**

tot

A young child.
Example: **The tot was sleepy.**

This is a summary of the Power Words the child has learned.
Have the child read them to you to make sure he or she has mastered them.

the	has	off
is	to	his
on	was	dog
as	of	for

Read more stories

| Instructions |

Say: "**Wow! You can now read stories using all the vowels. That's such a great accomplishment! Let's read one now.**"

Read a book

The child should read one book a day from the following list of Primary Phonics Set 1 books:

- "Ben Bug"
- "Meg"
- "Ted"
- "The Wig"
- "Ed"

I can read!

Certificate of Accomplishment

Presented to _____

Signed: _____

Date: _____